Tax Intelligence

Tax Intelligence

The Seven Habitual Tax Mistakes Made by Companies

Daniel N. Erasmus

BA (Law) B. Proc H. Dip Tax MTP (SAIT)
adjunct Professor of Law, Thomas Jefferson School of Law
Chairman and CEO TRM™ and www.Tax-Radar.com
Co-author IBFD Tax Risk
Management: from Risk to Opportunity

To order additional copies of this book, contact:
Xlibris Corporation
1-888-795-4274
www.Xlibris.com
Orders@Xlibris.com
68879

Contents

Chapter 1
Don't Be Reactive: Be Proactive 1

Chapter 4
Insular? Become More Transparent

Chapter 5
More Facts Resolve Tax Risks

Chapter 6
Internal Audits Fix Financial Accounting Problems

Preface

This TRM™ tax-Radar™ seven steps special report is based on over 120 lectures presented to many multinational corporations (MNEs) and smaller businesses (SMEs) looking to minimize one of the largest financial risks facing them: **tax**.

It looks at where they have failed to properly recognize the potential tax exposure they face. The case studies in this special report are very real and based on years of experience. The names, places, and specific details are not, so as to preserve the secrecy of the taxpayers.

One thing this special report will do for you is teach and guide you, step by step, that in matters of tax it is extremely dangerous not to be proactive. No matter what anyone says, tax is always and will always remain a large expense for any successful business. States will always look to their most successful taxpayers to collect 80% of the tax from the 20% most successful taxpayers. It makes commercial sense. The balance of tax officials' time will most probably be spent chasing after tax criminals, those who are blatant tax evaders and offenders. For you, who are reading this special report, I doubt you fall into this latter category; otherwise you would only have grabbed this special report if its title read *How to Evade Tax, Legally*!

IRSs around the world want to know that their actual cash flows from taxpayers are stable. A good guess is that about 20% of all taxpayers are those whom they rely on the most. If these 20% of taxpayers have devised a TRM™ process to ensure ongoing transparency and compliance through a self-audit process, the costs of collection and the costs of compliance are equally reduced, with an accurate result.

Disputes that may emerge will be limited to differences of opinion and interpretation where taxpayers have embarked on proactive tax planning, as opposed to arguing about shoddy unknown tax pitfalls.

Now it is for you to read on and open the door to proactive tax risk management (TRM™) and manage effectively one of the biggest financial risks in your business.

Prof. Daniel N. Erasmus
Jupiter, Florida, USA

The Purpose of This Special Report

To reach the following readers:	To communicate to businesses the importance of a proper (TRM™) process in their businesses so as to create certainty, minimal tax exposure, and full regulatory compliance with the seven TRM™ steps.
owners and CEOs	inform
BO/CFOs and their tax managers	persuade
boards of directors	call to action
audit committees	change attitudes
financial managers	argue
operations managers	summarize
transactions managers	recommend
tax advisors	propose

Disclaimer

All the information in this special report is written and provided for information purposes only and may not in any manner whatsoever be used as advice or as an opinion. Any attempt to use the information in this special report must not be made without obtaining appropriate advice from a qualified legal and/or other professional advisor to ensure full compliance with the laws and regulations of that country and to ensure that no damage, loss, or suffering may occur to the person seeking to use the information from this special report. The information in this special report cannot be relied upon in support of any contentions, arguments, or submissions made to any IRS authority or any other regulatory authority on any subject matter whatsoever. This list is not exhaustive. The author and publishers cannot be held responsible or liable for any damage, loss, or suffering whatsoever, by whomsoever, that may be occasioned by anyone influenced by or seeking to implement any of the information contained in this special report despite having taken appropriate legal and/or other professional advice.

What Are the Seven TRM™ Steps?

❑ **Step 1.** Taxpayers tend to be reactive to tax problems and tax risks. This will translate into additional tax exposure through the imposition of tax penalties and interest and lead to poor relationships with the Internal Revenue Service (IRS). Proactive tax risk management will eliminate the additional tax exposure, improve IRS relationships, and place control of the tax risk management process back in the hands of the business, and not the IRS. This then translates into a golden opportunity to develop an ongoing tax planning process, to keep tax exposures under control, and in a proactive manner. Refer to chapter 1.

❑ **Step 2**. Tax compliance departments in businesses try to cover their tax risk without outside professional assistance, except on a reactive basis. This contributes to step 1; tax risk management becomes reactive. By creating a tax team that participates proactively in the TRM™ process, the business is able to expand its tax risk cover from 40% to 100%. Refer to chapter 2.

❑ **Step 3**. Most businesses do not have a road map of how and where they are going with their tax risk management TRM™, other than blindly ensuring that they are "fully tax compliant." Without a properly formulated TRM™ strategy in place, the goals and objectives, and the manner of executing a TRM™ process so as to minimize tax risk, cannot be achieved properly. An extensive and fully maintained TRM™ strategy is what is required, with all potential tax risks summarized to be dealt with through defense files in the Tax Risk Matrix. Refer to chapter 3.

❑ **Step 4**. Insular tax compliance from an ivory tower (not getting into the trenches and your hands dirty to see where the real tax risks are) can only mean that tax compliance is probably at its lowest, despite attempts to ensure the opposite by businesses. All key stakeholders must be involved, from the CEO, BO/CFO, the board and the audit committee, the accountant to the legal team and tax advisors. Managers are often left on their own and expected to remain on top of tax compliance, law and regulatory changes, and the management of a complex series of relationships throughout the organization in order to get to the "tax truth" in many transactions, financial accounting, and operation areas. Their ability to be totally transparent, so as to limit ongoing exposure to the IRS deficiency assessments, is stifled by their lack of authority to access all key areas of the business and outside advice in areas that go beyond technical tax issues. Allowing transparency and connectivity into the mix turns the insular tax compliance problem around. Refer to chapter 4.

❑ **Step 5**. Lack of facts, facts, and more facts often leads to bad tax compliance and unnecessary mistakes that could have been avoided. Getting to the bottom of the facts takes time and effort and is the most important starting point in any TRM™ strategy implementation. Thereafter the technical expertise can be applied properly. Various business transactions illustrate this point time and time again, as businesses continuously fail to check the facts, check the advice, and then check the facts again. Refer to chapter 5.

❑ **Step 6**. Financial accounting supplies the numbers on which tax compliance is based. Simply relying on these numbers, as is usually the case with most managers and accountants, is not enough. Internal checking or audit procedures must be expanded to self-audit and checking the higher tax risk areas in a business, in order to self-expose any mistakes and noncompliance before the IRS does. This plays back into proactive tax risk management and the avoidance of unexpected and additional tax charges that may be crippling, if driven by the IRS. Refer to chapter 6.

❑ **Step 7**. Lack of communication between the accountant, or the manager responsible for tax, and the rest of the business, and merely processing numbers to compile tax returns, is the reason why tax compliance in most businesses only covers 40%

of the total tax risk in those businesses. The other 60% tax risk is hidden and can only be exposed through a systematic process of people-to-people communication, and not just through processing numbers. The one must verify the other. This calls for new communication systems to be implemented in the business to circumvent and put an end to the bad habit of limited people communication. Refer to chapter 7.

BBA Ltd. Decides to Go for TRM™

TAKE BBA LTD., part of the international Rialtry Group (a fictitious name but the facts are real) as an example. They faced a major tax audit on all fronts. The trigger had been an article in the *Exposé* magazine, citing them as having sneaked assets offshore under the radar screen without detection by the IRS, and now they were leaking huge sums of money to a tax-friendly jurisdiction, escaping significant tax charges in their country of effective management.

Four years later, they concluded their TRM™ process. The TRM™ process was heralded a great success by the board of directors of BBA Ltd., the Rialtry Group, and the IRS. Why?

There were no less than thirty key tax areas that required investigation and audit by the IRS. IRS audit teams were typically given one hundred man hours per key tax area to audit and then would be expected to deliver a result through revised assessments. Three thousand man hours would have been spent completing all the audits to arrive at a result for the IRS. This would have meant an equal, if not greater, amount of time and resource to be spent by BBA Ltd. With a very small tax department, they would have had to hire an extensive number of outside consultants at great expense.

What was at stake for BBA Ltd.? With hindsight now, they were facing a potential tax exposure of about $300m, plus penalties and interest of another $300m to be added. Had the IRS thrown three thousand man hours at the process they would have raised BBA Ltd. as a debtor of in the region of $600m. On the total man hours spent, the IRS would be looking to collect as much of that $600m as they could.

Again, with hindsight, and the conclusion of the TRM™ processes suggested in this special report, the IRS spent less than one hundred man hours. Because the taxpayer completed and controlled its own tax audit, internally, and self-disclosed to the IRS the outstanding amounts of tax that they had found definitely to be due to the IRS, it turned out that they had to pay much less than the $600m estimated. A host of potential transactions that the IRS may have been inclined to investigate, had they controlled the audit process, was cleared; and no revised assessments were issued, where under more adversarial circumstances the IRS may have treated the process otherwise. At the end of the day, a fraction of the $600m was raised in revised assessments.

For the taxpayer, what was the result? They faced tax charges up to $600m. This equated to three times more than the estimated income tax burden of the taxpayer for the year of assessment. Through a carefully implemented TRM™ process, and by being completely transparent, they reduced their feared tax exposure to a fraction of that amount. A substantial tax saving. Plus, had the IRS spent three thousand man hours, the taxpayer would have spent at least double that time hiring professionals to defend the legal actions of the IRS. The additional cost to BBA Ltd. time, effort, and expense would have equated to about $10m to bring the tax disputes to conclusion. The costs associated with the TRM™ process were one third of that amount.

All round, a significant saving of time, energy, and expense; and the result was satisfactory to all.

Acknowledgments

I am usually the one who comes up with the idea of a project like this one—the world's first to write and publish a tax risk management special report. Then, when I start, I realize that without assistance, it is not going to happen. There are a number of people who have assisted me in this project: Razaan Mohammed, my personal assistant, for diligently typing and retyping my drafts, and squiggles, my fellow professionals Terry Scott, Frances Louw, Kerry Watkin, and Allen Ross, for allowing me to use some of the material I asked them to write in the time leading up to the publication of this special report.

For the professional accounting firms Ernst & Young, Deloitte, KPMG, and PricewaterhouseCoopers for having such useful published tax risk management guidelines and snippets of information on tax risk management that has helped create a comprehensive and instructive piece of work. May your clients see the effort you have all put in toward creating this, not-so-new, area of risk management, which is so deserving of much more focus.

My wife, Marlize B. Erasmus, for supporting me in my many hours of work at the strangest of hours.

Gilbert Ferreira, for always being there and for giving me much-needed support in so many areas, allowing me the time to write.

And last, but not least, the editors, starting with Paul Jones, Gilbert Ferreira Sr., and Michael Fenton. And many more, too many to mention all of them!

Prof. Daniel Erasmus
Jupiter, Florida, USA
daniel@dnerasmus.com

TRM™ Dictionary

"**B**O/CFO**"** (which for a smaller business includes the business owner who acts as BO/CFO as well) means something like a UFO when it comes to **TRM™**, because many **BO/CFO**s (collectively referred to as BO/CFOs in this special report) often believe that tax is an "in due course" risk that should only be considered reactively. That's why this special report has been written, for you the **BO/CFO** to, hopefully, see otherwise and end up saving your business from an Enron-styled embarrassment. Nearly 30% of SOX 404 material weakness reports to the SEC show tax accounting as the problem. No other subject matter scores as high.

"**Defense files**" are the files that are built up after completing the Tax Risk Matrix that are ready to defend your business position if the IRS were to audit you.

"**Facts**" are mentioned frequently in this special report. Facts mean hard-core, material, tangible facts. Not assumptions! When **tax teams** get facts as part of the TRM process they are to uncover and obtain tangible documents containing information directly or indirectly relevant to the tax problem being investigated. This information may also be any information that has been stored in electronic format. In cases where tangible and intangible facts are not physically available, it may be necessary to track down persons who dealt with the aspect of the tax problem being investigated and to obtain from them, in written statement form, their best recollection of the facts. Although these written statements may not be evidence as good as the original source, the written statements will nevertheless prove to be very convincing where taxpayers are seeking to settle tax problems through a **soft outcomes** approach. In some cases these written statements may also prove to be useful evidence in a tax dispute, subject to the rules of evidence in the relevant tax jurisdiction.

"Forensic tax accountants" means a team of people skilled in conducting internal tax audits. For the smaller business in the tax-Radar™ program, this is covered.

"Legal privilege," in broad terms, is a special legal safeguard protecting the taxpayer in situations where any information disclosed to an attorney for advice is secret and confidential and may not be shared (under compulsion or otherwise) with an outside party where litigation was contemplated at the time the information is shared with the attorney. Any information disclosed under the **legal privilege** is privileged and protected and cannot be used in evidence (including civil disputes) against the taxpayer. To take advantage of this position, an attorney must be instructed in the **TRM** process and be appointed as the agent of the taxpayer. Any third parties contracted through that attorney, in the execution of duties on behalf of the taxpayer, will also be covered by the **legal privilege**. This includes other members of the **tax team**.

"Legal team" means a small team of lawyers (usually an attorney, with an assistant) skilled in **TRM™**, collating facts and evidence and possessing IRS-related negotiating experience. For the smaller business in the tax-Radar™ program, this is covered.

"Legitimate expectations" is the close neighbor of a right and is a legal doctrine derived from English law that should find application in many other jurisdictions. It is a legal doctrine entitling taxpayers to rely upon any practice or interpretation published by the IRS, as if these practice or interpretation publications are as binding as the law itself on the IRS, unless the content of these publications are clearly contrary to the law.

"Letter of findings" means the letter issued by IRS officials, prerevised deficiency notice giving detailed account and reasons for their particular findings after an IRS investigation or audit of a taxpayer's tax affairs. The taxpayer should always be given an opportunity to respond in writing to the **letter of findings**.

"Off-the-radar screen" means those **tax risk** areas determined after analyzing compliance, operational, transactional, and financial accounting areas under the **legal privilege**. This examination is usually done by the **tax team** and **forensic tax accountants** by interviewing key personnel in various business areas. Once identified, all relevant facts are compiled fully, including explanatory memoranda, opinions, views, agreements, and correspondence, and are submitted to the **legal team** and the **tax manager** for initial **tax risk** assessment and are then placed before the **tax team** for review, after the appropriate **opinion sign-off**, if necessary.

"On-the-radar screen" means a collection of all current tax issues and queries outstanding with the IRS and known to the IRS. These might, for example, be outstanding tax returns and all outstanding or current queries or audits with the IRS. After compiling an internal list with the relevant supporting information, the IRS should be requested to provide any outstanding items it might have. After drawing a comparison between the two lists, the outstanding **on-the-radar-screen** can be worked through by the **tax team** with the aim of achieving a **soft outcome** and an **IRS sign-off** with the appointed **IRS representative**. For the smaller business in the tax-Radar™ program, it is only necessary to complete the TRM™ Tax Risk Matrix.

"Opinion sign-off" means obtaining confirmatory written opinion, subject to **legal** privilege, by at least one tax specialist opining that the **tax risk** area has been properly and legitimately examined and arguably falls, within a reasonable interpretation of the tax law in question, in favor of the taxpayer. Such an opinion, if positive, can in some jurisdictions outside the USA be used in the future to stop any criminal prosecution (there being no criminal intent present), penalties, and interest. These are difficult to get—but not impossible if you have all the facts. In the USA beware of Circular 230!

"The IRS representative" means **the IRS representative** appointed as the contact point with IRS throughout the tax risk management **TRM™** process.

"The IRS sign-off" means a settlement agreement under the appropriate provisions of the tax statute to an agreed assessment, an advance tax ruling, or agreement with the IRS where you have successfully negotiated away a tax uncertainty.

"Soft outcomes" is the goal of the **legal team** in addressing contentious **tax risk** areas with the **IRS representative**. Here emphasis is placed on moving away from a potential dispute scenario to arrive at an agreed assessment, with minimal penalties and interest exposure. Any possibility of criminal prosecution falls away. This approach emanates from the taxpayer embarking upon a self-disclosure process with the IRS and an attempt by the **tax team** achieving an **IRS sign-off**.

"Tax manager" means the person in charge of tax compliance in the business who, after reading this special report, may acknowledge that another 60% tax liability is lurking in the historical annals of the business under transactions, financial accounting, and operations. If this person takes his or her work very seriously, he or she will attempt to convince the **BO/CFO** that a tax risk management **TRM™** strategy is appropriate, sooner rather than later.

"Tax risk" includes the meaning of "risk." Risk means "to expose to hazard; to endanger; to expose to the chance of injury or loss; to take the chances of" in accordance with the meaning ascribed to it in the compact edition of the *Oxford English Dictionary*. For the purposes of this special report it means identifying those areas in the business that give rise to potential financial loss when tax principles are applied to them, which must be quantified and managed to minimize that financial loss as any person would in the case of medical insurance, life insurance, trauma insurance, and property insurance. Most people are willing to pay for "insurance" to help minimize any financial loss that may emanate from the previously mentioned risks. For some unknown reason businesses do not budget or make allowance for spending funds on buying "insurance" in planning and implementing a TRM™ process in order to manage and minimize any financial loss that may flow from tax risk. Tax risk is the concept that must be recognized by business organizations in response to internal and external stakeholder demands, while continuing to meet business objectives and goals. Primarily it is a cautionary measure to avoid possible serious adverse financial consequences. It can be divided into two broad areas: internal and external **tax risk**.

External **tax risk** occurs through ongoing legislative and regulatory changes and new case law, giving rise to changes in application and interpretation of tax laws. Often businesses fail to keep abreast of these changes.

Internal **tax risk** can be classified as follows:

❑ transactional **tax risk**

❑ operational **tax risk**

❑ compliance **tax risk**

❑ financial accounting **tax risk**

❑ management **tax risk**

❑ reputational **tax risk**

By failing to effectively and efficiently manage transactional, operational, compliance, and financial accounting **tax risk**, management and reputational **tax risk** is also created.

"TRM™ Tax Risk Matrix" means the Tax Risk Matrix that is completed by the business at the first TRM™ strategy, setting out a summary of all the tax risks in the business, kept by tax-Radar™ off-site and updated by the business every month, or when a tax risk is resolved or a new one becomes apparent through the business accountant.

"tax-Radar™" is the system made available to you through www.tax-Radar.com and your accounting firm if you are a small business, providing you with the tax team, overseeing tax manager, legal team, and forensic tax accountants skill sets, making up your tax team, to assist you in compiling the Tax Risk Matrix, and providing you with complete tax representation from the time that the IRS indicates it wants to audit you until the matter is completed in the tax court or by negotiation, subject to the terms and conditions of the tax-Radar™ mandate signed by you.

"TRM™ strategy" means the **tax risk management (TRM™) strategy** for the business, updated at least every six months, as described in chapter 3 below.

"**Tax team**" means the following persons involved with the planning, implementation, and execution of **TRM™** process. The **tax team** usually includes

❑ the **BO/CFO** or business owner in a smaller business,

❑ the **tax manager**,

❑ a representative from each operating division or subsidiary,

❑ the **legal team**,

❑ a representative of the **forensic tax accountants**,

❑ a representative of the auditors, and

❑ a representative of the current tax advisors,

acting as tax steering committee for the execution of the **TRM™** process. Sometimes the latter two representatives only get involved once all initial problem areas have been identified. They will make recommendations, via the **BO/CFO** or business owner, to the board of directors, through the audit committee. Their initial function will be to determine (together with representatives from each operating division) the **TRM™ strategy** to assist in determining their tax risk areas. Thereafter the implementation and execution of issues arising are carried out with regular reporting to the audit committee. For the smaller business in the tax-Radar™ program, this is covered.

"**Tax Query Questionnaire or TQQ**" means the set of questions set out below. All or some of these questions are to be given to the IRS to complete before providing them with any information (other than the appropriate tax return) where they make a request, without giving complete details what the inquiry is about, or for, and whether or not the information, documents, or things to be supplied are mandatory. The **TQQ** must emanate from the **tax manager**. Any IRS response must be reviewed by the **tax manager**, under appropriate circumstances, with the assistance of the **legal team**. The **TQQ** will ensure that proper administrative procedures are adhered to by the IRS. For a list of the authorities supporting these questions please email Prof. Daniel N. Erasmus daniel@dnerasmus.com. The **TQQ** is as follows (please take note of the disclaimer at the end of these questions):

❑ State the authority, giving the specific sections of the legislation, for the solicitation of the information that you require.

❑ State whether the disclosure of the requested information is mandatory or voluntary. If mandatory, why?

❑ State what penalties may/will result from noncompliance in furnishing the information you have requested.

❑ State the principle and specific purpose for which the information requested is to be used in any and all capacities.

❑ State the routine uses which may be made of the requested information or any other use to be made of the requested information.

❑ State the effect on the taxpayer for not providing the commissioner or its officials with the information requested.

❑ Explain and show that the investigation involved is of the kind authorized by legislation.

❑ Explain how and why the demand for information is not too vague and broad in scope.

❑ Explain and show that the information sought is relevant or material as a lawful subject of this inquiry.

❑ Explain why and how the investigation is pursuant to legitimate purposes.

❑ Explain why and how the inquiry for information may be relevant to the purposes.

❑ Show and prove that the information is not already in the possession of the commissioner or his officials or cannot be obtained from other sources.

❑ Show and prove that the commissioner or his officials have determined that this further examination is necessary.

❑ Show and prove that all other administrative steps, as required by law and your practice, have been followed.

❑ Show and prove that after initial investigation, the commissioner or his officials have determined that a further examination is necessary and warranted.

❑ Show and prove that the taxpayer has been properly notified that further examination is necessary.

❑ State exact reasons in detail for the examination of the specific year/s for which information is requested.

❑ State whether there is any misconception and/or a mistake in the tax return for the specific year/s in which the information is requested.

❑ State exactly where the mistake lies, or if in fact, that one exists.

❑ Specify exactly which items of income or expenses are in question on the tax return, if any.

❑ State why the specific income and/or expense item is in question or needs to be examined, if any.

❑ Explain why and what issue in law or fact is being questioned.

❑ State the name, address, and telephone number of any person or persons informing you of any questions or concerns involved in any item or tax return or any activity of the taxpayer.

❑ State exactly what was said, either verbally and/or written concerning any item, tax return, or activity of the taxpayer by any person(s) informing or directing you to conduct an examination directly or indirectly.

- ❑ State and prove that the taxpayer is not being subjected to an examination based on/or for any political, ideological, harassment, pressure, tactic, or bad faith purpose and is not being singled out for prosecution as an example to other taxpayers for any reason.

- ❑ State and explain why the examination cannot and will not amount to an inquisition or arbitrary inquiry on the part of the commissioner or its officials.

- ❑ State and explain why you feel that the taxpayer is not being subjected to unnecessary examination or investigation.

- ❑ State the exact methods used, either past or present, to gather information concerning this taxpayer and whether information was gathered through the use of unusual means.

- ❑ State whether the verification of specific deductions would be the limited scope of the examination.

- ❑ State whether the commissioner or his officials would be prejudiced against the taxpayer who arranges his affairs to minimize tax as the law permits.

- ❑ Show and prove to the taxpayer how the commissioner or his officials have jurisdiction over any subject matter concerning the taxpayer or the parties that the taxpayer conducted business with.

- ❑ Show and prove that the commissioner or his officials have established sufficient jurisdictional facts to bring the taxpayer within the ambit of the legislation so as to shift the onus of proof to the taxpayer.

*Disclaimer: All the information in this special report, including the TQQ above, is provided for information purposes only and not as advice or as an opinion, and any attempt to use this information or these questions must not be made without the involvement and advice of the **legal team** or another appropriate professional advisor.*

"**TRM™**" means **tax risk management TRM™** as described in this special report.

"**Appendices**"—the following documents form part of this special report and are available for download at http://www.taxriskmanagement.com/7habits and http://www.tax-Radar.com:

❏ TRM™ Tax Risk Matrix Template

❏ Tax Risk TRM™ Policies and Procedures Special Report

❏ Tax Risk Review Template

❏ TRM™ Web Interface

"**Final Note**" the word "assessment" and "assessments" is used in this special report. This includes a deficiency notice in the USA. Assessment is the term used in many other jurisdictions to describe a similar event to a deficiency notice. It should be noted that this special report is addressed to an audience wider than the US reader. Many of the examples and case studies are based on interactions with tax authorities other than the IRS. However, the IRS has been used as the principal tax authority in this special report.

Chapter 1
Don't Be Reactive: Be Proactive

Wikipedia, the free online encyclopedia, defines the word "proactive" as originally coined by the psychiatrist Victor Frankl ... and ...

popularized in the business press in Stephen Covey's 7 Habits of Highly Effective People ... and ...

the word has come to mean "to act before a situation becomes a source of confrontation or crisis" vs. "after the fact."

Executive Summary

BEING PROACTIVE WITH tax risk management TRM™ requires decisive steps to be taken by the BO/CFO, with the tax manager. The steps include forming a tax team under the leadership of the legal team to ensure legal privilege, plotting a TRM™ strategy, and then determining what the on- and off-the-radar screen issues are. The aim of the process is to eliminate the tax risks before they become disputes, obtaining resolution through the IRS representative sign-off, moving toward a soft outcomes solution to any TRM™ issues. With the completion of the TRM™ process, the taxpayer's ability to tax plan into the future increases proportionately.

Introduction

THIS CHAPTER DEALS with TRM™ Step 1.

Taxpayers tend to be reactive to tax problems and tax risks. This will translate into additional tax exposure through the imposition of tax penalties and interest and lead to poor relationships with the

1

IRS. Proactive tax risk management will eliminate the additional tax exposure, improve IRS relationships, and place control of the tax risk management process back in the hands of the business, and not the IRS. This then translates into a golden opportunity to develop an ongoing tax planning process, to keep tax exposures under control, and in a proactive manner.

Incriminating Evidence

"JUDGE, MAY I present the overwhelming evidence that tilts the balance of the probability scale in favor of the proposition that tax is one of the most significant risks facing businesses, and that, viewed from different perspectives, the clear conclusion to be drawn is that corporate officers display a *laissez-faire* attitude toward the inherent danger tax risk poses to the fortunes of shareholders and business owners, despite an attempt by numerous regulators to arrest the problem."

In an online survey conducted on what were the main causes of material weakness disclosures to the SEC in the USA under SOX 404 (see chapter 8), nearly 30% of all reports showed problems with tax accounting. The highest material weakness!

FIN 48 and IFRS (see chapter 8) require companies to determine their tax liabilities and disclose these in their financial statements, despite the fact that the actual liability may only arise in the future. Failure to quantify such a tax liability will result in qualified or inaccurate financial statements. This in turn will cause repercussions under SOX 404 for companies trading their stocks on the USA stock markets.

A large international accounting firm tax risk specialist has suggested in a paper by one of its leading tax risk specialists that as much as 75% of businesses tax risk remains outside the accepted realm of tax compliance.

This was the case a few years ago. Well, the regulators got their way, and it seems that big business is complying. So the problem for small businesses is that IRS audits are now being focused on smaller businesses.

The Degree of Inattention to Tax Risk Management (TRM™)

IN AN ONLINE TRM™ survey conducted by over 167 member businesses through www.taxriskmanagement.com, the results showed that both small and big businesses are generally not on top of their tax risks, and there are many. To see the up-to-date survey results please go to www. taxriskmanagement.com

The evidence is overwhelming enough to convince any CEO, BO/CFO, board of directors, audit committee, or tax manager that tax risk should be a major concern for most businesses, requiring proactive attention on an ongoing basis.

Tax, if managed reactively, will remain a dangerous problem, difficult to manage when liabilities are unexpectedly uncovered.

The Case of K Products Ltd.

THE CASE OF K Products Ltd. illustrates the difference between reactive and proactive tax risk management.

K Products Ltd. had inherited a number of merger transactions over the years that the IRS, through one of their special investigations units, had audited and now decided to issue revised tax assessments totaling hundreds of millions of dollars, including penalty tax and interest. The outside advisory team that had dealt with the process had advised K Products Ltd. to keep the interaction with the IRS to a minimum and not to divulge or disclose too many facts, as the opportunity would arise in the future when the matter went to tax court. As a result, many opportunities that existed prior to the raising of the revised assessments were lost in convincing the IRS that nothing was wrong with some of the merger transactions. The IRS had also failed to follow certain important legal procedural rules in arriving at their decisions, which could have resulted in any steps taken by them to raise the revised tax assessments being overturned.

As a result, the revised tax assessments were raised, and K Products Ltd. now had to face the music of raising formal written objections against the revised tax assessments and to fight off the tax collection authorities, who were now attempting to extract the hundreds of millions of dollars out of them, pending the finalization of the tax court case at some uncertain point in the future. In fact, shortly after the assessments were raised, K Products Ltd. ended up paying a fairly large "goodwill" sum, pending the outcome of the dispute in the tax court. It was clear that the IRS would attempt to extract more money in the near future from them.

To add fuel to the fire, the media had also been given a statement on the tax position of K Products Ltd., and investor analysts were concerned.

The entire process had been followed in a reactive manner. Each time the IRS took a step, the advisory team waited then reacted cautiously, without making too many disclosures for fear of causing some advantage in favor of the IRS. The result: the process quickly followed the usual route to revised tax assessments, with K Products Ltd. being placed under pressure to enter the formal tax dispute arena and start paying the revised assessed taxes, as the amounts were now final debts due to the State, until the revised tax assessments were overturned by a tax court at a later stage.

Shortly after this gut-wrenching process had come to a head, the BO/CFO of the company decided to try a different approach for the remainder of the tax risks inside K Products Ltd., which they were also still trying to handle, with imminent revised assessments about to be issued.

An immediate tax team was formed, comprising the BO/CFO, the tax manager, the current outside tax advisors, and a new legal team, qualified to handle a TRM™ process of this nature.

The first meeting was called, and all the tax issues were tabled and summarized in tabular form. The matters were ranked according to priority.

Time lines were attached to each of the tax risk items, with a summary of what had to be done to bring the matters to finality. The capital tax, penalties, and interest for each tax risk item were determined, subject to legal privilege, under the guidance of the legal team. One of the first strategies that would be embarked upon would be to minimize any penalty or interest exposure to the IRS. This required careful preparation, drafting the suitable presentation to the IRS and involving opinion sign-off, soft outcomes, and IRS sign-off.

The roles and responsibilities of the various tax team members were carefully determined.

The first task was to make contact with a neutral individual in the IRS to go and see the IRS representative. An agenda was agreed upon, which included the historical dispute issues, regarding the current on-the-radar screen issues, and the proposed way to go forward. At the same time, the IRS representative was asked to determine from their systems all outstanding tax returns and tax queries that appeared on their internal system. This would be used as the first item to be cleared with the IRS to show good faith on the part of K Products Ltd.

The first meeting took place. The result was the handing over of a list of outstanding tax issues to K Products Ltd., an agreement on the method to be adopted in arriving at conclusions of tax audits before revised tax assessments were raised, and the fact that the historical disputes would be dealt with separately by the tax advisors who were originally involved. One important concession was agreed upon: the fact that K Products Ltd. was embarking on an overhauling of all its TRM™ issues was acknowledged by the IRS, all payments on revised assessments and the issuing of revised tax assessments would be suspended, as K Products Ltd. was given a fair and reasonable opportunity to systematically work through its tax risk issues with the IRS. It was agreed in principle that soft outcomes would be sought ultimately, with the view to obtaining the IRS sign-off on any disputes that may arise, without resorting to unnecessary litigation. It was also agreed that the PNAL principle, if any revised assessments were raised, would be suspended until the IRS sign-off took place at the end of a tax dispute. This meant that any payments under revised tax assessments would be suspended until the final conclusion of the tax dispute.

It was also agreed that the TQQ questions (see the "TRM™ Dictionary") could be issued by the taxpayer on any investigations conducted by the IRS, to ensure there was proper procedural compliance by them. Any audit would also end with the appropriate letter of findings, before a revised assessment was issued by the IRS.

A structured and fair TRM™ process, with the participation of the IRS, could now be embarked upon.

The next step in the process was to get the tax team together so as to formulate an overall TRM™ strategy for the company to take care of the historical, current, and future tax risk issues, including any off-the-radar screen tax risk issues.

Eighteen months later, K Products Ltd. had paid no more revised tax assessment monies. No further revised assessments had been raised, and matters were well under way toward bringing most of the on-the-radar screen issues to a conclusion with IRS sign-off. In appropriate places the IRS had issued letters of findings. In addition to this, a number of proposed tax audits had been done away with and postponed, taking immediate pressure off K Products Ltd. to commit more resources to the IRS's demands. K Products Ltd. was now also able to finally start collating and analyzing information on some of its off-the-radar screen issues, under legal privilege, without fear that the IRS would demand sensitive information before it was due to be disclosed to them at the conclusion of the process.

The final goal was also about to be reached: high and lower level settlement discussions with the IRS to reach soft outcomes on most of the outstanding tax issues without resorting to tax litigation. The company was also properly prepared for the conclusion of the TRM™ process on this basis, having researched and investigated each tax issue thoroughly through the tax team and the TRM™ process.

The specific TRM™ processes referred to in this case study will be discussed in greater detail throughout this special report.

Basic Tax Compliance Is Not Enough

MOST TAXPAYERS TRY to keep their affairs in order, but what they do not realize is that basic tax compliance is not enough. Invariably there are so many other tax-related issues which taxpayers do not recognize as risk areas. Since they have never received any queries from the IRS, taxpayers may believe those tax risk areas have not been identified and the IRS has either accepted or overlooked them. This is an assumption which taxpayers should never make, and yet it is probably one of the most common mistakes. Generally speaking, taxpayers are reactive when it comes to dealing with the IRS; and it is this attitude which costs them more money in the long run, with additional tax penalties and interest.

Proactive Tax Risk Management TRM™

SO WHAT SHOULD taxpayers do? The answer lies in the planning, implementation, and execution of a tax risk management TRM™ process which is proactive. The idea is not to be reactive and to see tax as some historic event. Control of the tax environment commences with advanced planning—before the commencement of a business transaction, financial accounting event, or operation. Failure to roll out such a TRM™ could result in negative tax consequences which cannot be changed back in time.

The Tax Team

THE FIRST STEP in the TRM™ process requires the appointment of a tax team. For the small business the solution lies in joining the tax-Radar™ program. For big business, this team will most likely consist of the BO/

CFO, the tax manager, a representative from each operational division in the business, independent advisors from the taxpayer's existing tax advisors, forensic tax accountants, and a legal team skilled in guiding and participating in the TRM™ process, providing the necessary legal privilege protection to sensitive tax areas being investigated. Collectively, the tax team will in turn report to the audit committee.

The Tax Risk Management TRM™ Strategy

> *"Tax teams must have appropriate tax risk management TRM policies and procedures in place, included in a Tax Risk Management TRM Strategy.*
>
> *The Tax Risk Management TRM Strategy should address the functions of the tax team and their integration with other divisions in the business, with the assistance of the legal team, forensic tax accountants, auditors, and current tax advisors."*
>
> *For a TRM Policies and Procedures Manual go to www.tax-Radar.com*

THE TAX TEAM'S initial function will be to determine (together with representatives from each operating division) the TRM™ strategy to assist in establishing the key risk areas.

One of the first events after the formation of the tax team is a TRM™ strategy for the business, to document this strategy for historical, current, and future tax risk issues. This will be dealt with in more detail in chapter 3.

For the small business, this process takes place through the completion of the Tax Risk Matrix with the accountant for the business.

The IRS Representative

THEREAFTER, FOR BIG BUSINESS the relevant IRS representative needs to be identified as the point of contact between the tax team and the IRS. It is with this person that all communication, outside the submission of usual tax returns, will take place. The IRS representative will be the recipient of all other correspondence, and the taxpayer's representatives are to liaise with this person in order to build a solid working relationship and address its tax affairs into the future. They will also be responsible for providing the on-the-radar screen tax issues to the taxpayers at inception of the TRM™ process. In time to come, they will facilitate the IRS sign-off is the tax team moving toward a soft outcomes solution to any tax issues.

In the case of the small business, this step is not necessary.

On-the-Radar Screen Tax Issues

THE BUSINESS, AND in the case of big business, the IRS should be requested to prepare a list of all outstanding tax issues pertaining to the taxpayer. These outstanding tax issues (returns and queries with the IRS) will be added and matched to all the outstanding tax returns and queries list compiled by the business. These listed items are referred to as being **on-the-radar tax risk issues**. When the tax-Radar™ program is implemented for the small business, the accountant will compile the on-the-radar tax risk issues in the Tax Risk Matrix.

Off-the-Radar Screen Tax Issues

ALL HISTORICAL TAX issues identified in the business as being problematical, but not on-the-radar screen, must be highlighted for internal tax audit purposes. These are the business's off-the-radar screen issues. Typical historical problem areas will be indirect tax supporting documents (reflecting compliant invoices), tax and accounting provisions, structured finance transactions, and transfer pricing transactions.

Being off-the-radar does not mean these items should be ignored. If anything, the TRM™ strategy should cater for these issues in advance, before the IRS attempts to challenge something. In this way, the taxpayer will be well prepared to handle any IRS queries. Because the tax team is working under the guidance of the legal team, the process will be subject to legal privilege.

Gathering the Facts

THE NEXT STEP in the TRM™ process is to obtain all the relevant facts surrounding both on-the-radar screen and off-the-radar screen issues. This involves procuring agreements, both draft and final, memoranda, minutes of meetings, resolutions, opinions, and correspondence (both verbal and written). This is often the most time-consuming part, but it is also the most crucial because so many times a case is won on the evidence which is contained in witness testimony and supporting documentation.

A good lawyer will tell you, "Show me a good set of facts, and I'll find the law to get you out of the pickle!"

Many transactions entered into by the taxpayer involve several role players and generate significant volumes of documentation which then end up dispersed in the possession of various persons. Taxpayers should be mindful that this is an inevitable consequence, and so if they failed to do so during the negotiation stage, then they should ensure the factual procurement is done as soon as possible. This entails obtaining every single piece of documentation, whether the taxpayer believes it to be relevant or not. Should the IRS at a later stage request all the evidence, as it is entitled to do, it is the responsibility of the tax team to determine what is irrelevant and need not be disclosed. It is prudent to conduct this exercise sooner rather than later because taxpayers find that with the lapse of time, documents are misplaced and key players move on and fail to inform others or recall where the documentation was stored.

Analysis of the Facts and Opinion Sign-Off

ONCE ALL THE facts have been compiled, the tax team will be equipped to consider the issue holistically and determine the tax implications, if any. Where uncertainty or contentious issues exist, it is best to obtain expert advice. Here opinion sign-off must take place. An objective opinion is useful for a number of reasons; firstly it can confirm the taxpayer's treatment is correct. Secondly, if the taxpayer's manner of implementation or compliance is not in accordance with legislation, the advice could provide the correct guidance, thus affording the taxpayer an opportunity to rectify its conduct. Thirdly, seeking an opinion will always demonstrate good faith and the absence of intention to evade or postpone the payment of tax. But make sure you give the tax advisor all the relevant facts and beware of Circular 230 in the USA. It is essential that any opinion obtained is under the guidance of the legal team to ensure that the opinion is subject to legal privilege.

Resolution through the IRS Sign-Off

THE AIM OF the TRM™ process is to address all the taxpayer's outstanding tax issues in order to resolve them expeditiously with the aid of an amicable interactive relationship with the IRS and ultimately an IRS sign-off. If this process is managed properly, the result is a competent tax team who are at all times on top of the taxpayer's affairs and aware of its exposure. Insofar as there is tax exposure, the tax team will have followed the correct measures in minimizing these exposures and will be equipped to advance appropriate submissions to the IRS for settlement and the IRS sign-off toward a soft outcomes solution.

The Ever-Present IRS

ULTIMATELY, NEITHER THE IRS nor the businesses tax problems are going to go away. If these problems are acknowledged and the right people (the tax team) are put in charge to handle these tax issues proactively, the business will be in a much better position to manage the tax risks to its benefit than the unprepared taxpayer that is caught off guard.

Proactive Tax Risk Management TRM™ Checklist

TO ACHIEVE A proactive implementation of the TRM™ process, the business needs to focus on the following issues and tasks:

❑ Commit to go beyond basic tax compliance.

❑ Get the buy-in of the business owner, the CEO, the BO/CFO, the board of directors, and the audit committee.

❑ Appoint a tax team or participate in the tax-Radar™ program.

❑ Constitute a reporting structure to the audit committee or accountant in small businesses.

❑ Set a TRM™ strategy date.

❑ Communicate with an IRS representative, if required, under guidance from the tax team, or the accountant.

❑ Determine the on-the-radar screen tax issues.

❑ Meet with the IRS representative.

❑ Agree with the IRS representative that the TQQ will be answered, that letters of finding will be issued, and that soft outcomes will be sought.

❑ Set regular meeting dates with the IRS representative.

❑ Determine the off-the-radar screen tax issues.

❑ Gather all relevant facts.

❑ Analyze all the facts.

❑ Get specialist technical advice and opinion sign-off.

❑ Determine the best path to resolving the issue, including a soft outcomes resolution through an IRS representative sign-off.

Proactive Planning into the Future and Tax Planning

"Tax planning is an area of increased sensitivity from Listed Exchange Bodies, tax authorities, investors, investor analysts and shareholders.

Tax Teams must have appropriate tax risk management TRM ™ policies and procedures in place (a Tax Strategy).

The Tax Strategy should address the functions of the Tax Team and their integration with other divisions in the business, with the assistance of the Legal Team, Forensic Tax Accountants, Auditors and Current Tax Advisors.

It should be remembered that tax risk aversion does not mean tax planning and opportunity aversion. Managing tax risks does not mean eliminating tax risk.

The challenge is to transform risk aversion into risk assessment—to identify and communicate the risks that are inherent in the business and enterprise environment, and then exploit opportunities within the corporate governance environment."

Source: Ernst & Young

PROACTIVE TRM™ COMMENCES with a change of attitude from the top down in the business. The change is that tax must not be seen as some reactive process, where tax is seen as a historic event. This entails proactive tax planning. Control of a business's tax environment commences with tax planning—before the commencement of a business transaction, financial accounting event, or day-to-day operations. Failure to do this will mean a direct connection to a potentially negative tax consequence, which cannot be changed after the fact.

In fact, proactive tax risk management starts with tax planning.

Legal Privilege Persists

ANY INFORMATION IN any way associated with the TRM™ process or "tax planning" may draw the attention of IRS assessors. It's human nature. In any event, they will also ask to have sight of anything remotely attached to any concept of "tax planning," as this becomes the doorway to any IRS fishing expedition, assisting them in identifying key tax risk areas in the business.

For all the above reasons, any tax planning should be done under the umbrella of the legal team and subject to legal privilege. For this reason as a precaution, all "tax planning" documents, draft or otherwise, must be addressed to the business's attorneys of record (in the legal team) and marked "subject to legal privilege."

This then becomes a safe-haven starting point, to ensure that any snooping IRS assessors will discover that they cannot have access to any information, documents, or things that are subject to the legal privilege. In any event, any preliminary planning information is usually irrelevant to any IRS investigation if the transaction was never implemented or if the final form of the transaction is different from what it looked like in the early stages of planning the transaction. But in the absence of the "subject to legal privilege" stamp, many employees fielding IRS questions may end up providing some of these irrelevant documents, thereby opening the door to an IRS fishing expedition. Avoid this at all costs.

Despite tax planning being a very important process for any business, it can give rise to unnecessary risks if not managed properly.

Tax planning must fall within the overall tax strategy with the support and knowledge of the business owner, CEO, CFO, board of directors, and audit committee.

> *"An important issue for a board and CEO is to consciously decide the position they wish to take on tax planning, rather than have it made for them by others."*
>
> Source: Michael Carmodey, Australian Commissioner on Taxation, January 2004

How Big Is the Tax Planning Opportunity?

THE TAX PLANNING opportunity is especially big if all your businesses on-the-radar screen and off-the-radar screen issues have been resolved.

The business can feel comfortable that it has nothing to hide. It can now focus on the positive side of proactive tax planning.

Disclosing Tax Planning Opportunities?

REMEMBER THE KEY tax risk areas that the IRS will look for in executing any tax plan. For instance, where the business's tax rate drops significantly overnight, the IRS will wonder why. If there is a tax refund, expect a visit from the IRS, and be prepared to explain why.

> *"The most important rule in tax planning: do not lightly allow tax considerations to distort a commercial transaction."*
>
> Source: Prof. E. B. Broomberg

So as to ensure stability and continuity of your improved tax status with the IRS, get an advance tax ruling on any proposed transaction that may result in a tax reduction, if possible. Obviously, the essence of the proposed transaction must be driven by commercial factors, where tax is a secondary consideration. That way, no one can say that there has been any nondisclosure, misrepresentation, or fraud. The advance tax ruling request will contain all the key and relevant information, with a request for the appropriate binding ruling.

If an advance tax ruling is not possible, ensure proper and full disclosure of the transaction in the next tax return and in any documentation that, by law, must be submitted to the IRS disclosing a "reportable transaction."

Where Do the Tax Planning Opportunities Lie?

THE OPPORTUNITIES WILL present themselves through the ongoing investigation into the potential tax risk areas in the business and through the constant communication between members of the tax team, provided their attitude is programmed to look out for potential tax planning opportunities. The culture in the tax team environment should not only be pitched at uncovering negative tax risks but honed in recognizing positive tax risks, or opportunities, as well. The tax team should continuously consider tax planning issues and objectives at their regular monthly meetings.

Tax Planning Checklist

TO ACHIEVE INTEGRATION between the tax team and the business so as to maximize tax planning opportunities in the TRM™ process, the business needs to focus on the following issues and tasks:

❑ Has the business undergone an IRS audit in the last five years?

❑ Has the business not conducted an internal tax audit in the last twelve months?

Has the business conducted major transactions in the last five years, including mergers, acquisitions, asset disposals, management buyouts, and the like which have not undergone a posttransaction legal and tax audit?

Are dividend yields decreasing, and how can tax planning reverse this?

Has an educational analysis of recent tax law, regulation, and practice changes as they impact on the business, both historically and in the future, taken place?

Is the tax rate high when compared with competitors in the same industry and in other countries where the business operates in, and how can this be remedied?

❑ Has a "benchmarking" industry comparison tax table identifying areas of tax leakage, such as unutilized tax deductions, losses, and allowances, or opportunities to classify revenue as capital, or suspend tax changes until later, taken place?

❑ Has the legal structure of the business and the details of business financing been reviewed?

❑ What are the trends contributing to the business tax charge?

❑ Has an initial diagnosis of the reasons for the current effective tax rate been prepared?

❑ Has each potential point of present taxation cost and the effect on the value of the business been determined?

❑ Has the business's effective tax rate been managed, and has it been considered what should be the target level, with time periods to achieve this?

❑ What value can be obtained taking tax risks?

❑ How does this affect the effective rate of tax?

❑ What costs are saved in reducing tax risks vs. what are the costs of resources to manage tax planning opportunities?

❑ What is the broad understanding of tax morality vs. rule of law, risks, and opportunities?

❑ Has management looked to legitimately generate profits in low tax jurisdictions or in a tax loss entity, mindful of strict antitax avoidance legislation?

❑ Have methods been identified to extract profits from high tax jurisdictions?

❑ Have methods been identified to place expenses and debt in high tax jurisdictions?

❑ Can tax payment dates be deferred?

❑ Have fiscal and other business incentives been used?

❑ Have benefits of double tax agreements been maximized?

❑ Have foreign tax credits been optimized?

❑ Have effective hedging and repatriation strategies been exploited?

❑ Have tax risks been insulated?

Source: E. Mascall

"Isolate and identify each of the several factors that give rise to a tax liability, then consider one or more ways of neutralizing those factors."

Source: Prof. E. B. Broomberg

Where Is the Tax Planning Done?

THE STARTING POINT of both aspects of tax planning, negative and positive, is the tax risk management TRM™ strategy which will plot the on- and off-the-radar screen tax issues, with a plan to seek tax planning opportunities in the future.

Who Is Ultimately Responsible for the Tax Planning?

THE ULTIMATE RESPONSIBILITY lies with the business owner, the CEO, and the BO/CFO who should empower the tax team to get on with it. They are responsible for creating the best shareholder value possible, under the circumstances. They cannot do so if their tax planning is defective.

They, in turn, must be guided by the board, audit committee, and risk committee. These entities, in turn, obtain all relevant information from the tax team.

> "Tax liability is determined as follows, for tax planning purposes:
>
> - Quality of the amount (capital, dividend, nonresident, etc.)
> - Factor of time (conditions present to delay receipt or accrual)
> - Fact of incidence (who is the person that pays the tax)
> - Source (residency)"
>
> Source: Prof. E. B. Broomberg

The ultimate aim of implementing the tax planning strategies is to increase shareholder value.

The key information required to put a tax planning process into action emanates from a culmination of the whole tax risk management TRM™ process. It starts with getting the tax affairs of the business in order. All tax affairs. Followed by getting the IRS sign-off on all known tax risk areas, except those that do not require it (because defense files are sufficient), ending in the regular function of in-house tax audits and annual tax strategy sessions.

Lastly, apply a proactive approach in tax planning to any anticipated changes emanating from a proposed change in legislation, the IRS practice, and recent case law. This requires an analysis of the changes as they impact on the business, both historically and going into the future.

> Judge Learned Hand of the USA wrote,
>
> "[A]ny one may so arrange his affairs that his taxes shall be as low as possible; he is not bound to choose that pattern which will best pay the Treasury; there is not even a patriotic duty to increase one's taxes."
>
> Source: Helvering v. Gregory (1934 CCH POVA 9180)

"Areas to audit to expose any tax risks:

- *Inbound logistics—materials handling, warehousing*
- *Operations—turning new materials into finished products*
- *Outbound logistics—order processing and distribution*
- *Marketing and sales—communications and pricing*
- *Service—installation and after-sales service*
- *Procurement service—purchasing and supply*
- *Technology development—know-how, procedures, and skills*
- *Human resource management—recruitment, promotion, appraisal, reward, and development*
- *Firm infrastructure—general and quality management, finance, planning."*

Source: M. Porter

Chapter 2

Not on Your Own: Create a Tax Team

> *"The shortest and best way to make your fortune is to let people see clearly that it is in their interests to promote yours."*
>
> Source: Jean de La Bruyere, 1645–1696

Executive Summary

THE IRS is one of the biggest partners of a business each year. It is mysterious that people do not invest more into allowing themselves to understand and deal with this silent partner more effectively and efficiently. By creating an environment within a business that assesses tax risk, every other part of the business is potentially enriched through the new transparent processes that are implemented, with the participation of a number of key persons working together. It is illogical as to why businesses do not invest in creating a tax team that ends up saving the business significant tax exposure into the future.

Empowering the tax team with the support and the easy flow of communication within the business is also vital. The tax team must become a vital cog of the business and be made up of people empowered with knowledge, not only on the law, but the knowledge of what exactly is going on within the business through the implementation of an effective and efficient TRM™ process. An efficient communication process must also be implemented in the business.

Introduction

IN THE PREVIOUS chapter the importance of proactive tax risk management was discussed. Guidelines were given as to how proactive tax risk management can be achieved.

This chapter deals with TRM™ Step 2.

Tax compliance departments in businesses try to cover their tax risk without outside professional assistance, except on a reactive basis. This contributes to TRM™ Step 1; tax risk management becomes reactive. By creating a tax team that participates proactively in the TRM™ process, the business is able to expand its tax risk cover from 40% to 100%. Small businesses will have the benefit of enrolling in the tax-Radar™ program offered by their accountants where they will have a tax team on their side 24/7 to guide them through the Tax Risk Matrix process and to assist them immediately the IRS attempts to audit the small business, through to final representation in the tax court, or negotiation, subject to the terms and conditions of the tax-Radar™ mandate.

What the Doctor Ordered

IN THE LEGAL profession there is an old adage: "He who represents himself has a fool for a client." Clearly an accurate statement based on real and hard experience of lawyers. Similarly, there is the danger when sickness and disease hit our bodies we tend to become self-diagnosticians. We either think the worst or worry ourselves to distraction or inaction. Alternatively we try and ignore the symptoms in the expectation that they will eventually go away! When they don't, only then do we drag ourselves off to the expert, the doctor or specialist, and get an expert diagnosis of the problem so that we can get treated and secure the necessary relief, often after much irreparable damage has been done.

In simple terms we become very subjective in our outlook, and all sense of reasonability and objectivity fall off-the-radar screen. We end up encountering more problems, difficulties, or setbacks that could so easily have been avoided had we simply taken the necessary expert advice at the very beginning, when the problems or symptoms first arose or appeared. Another old adage comes to mind—"Prevention is better than cure."

Is Tax Different?

WE OFTEN MAKE the same mistakes when we approach our tax affairs be it in business or even on a personal level. We try to handle our own tax affairs and clearly lack the necessary skills or expertise to handle them properly or adequately. When tax problems arise we ignore them in the hope that they will go away or not be detected, or we panic to such a degree that we are paralyzed and hope that the sword of Damocles in the hands of the IRS will not fall on us.

It goes without saying that in handling tax affairs, prevention of problems is far better than trying to find a cure or solution for them when they do rear their "ugly" heads.

Tax, to say the least, is a vast and very complex subject to which we are all subservient once we enter the arena of business or start earning an income. The greater the earnings we derive from our employment or the greater the profits we make in business, the greater the desire and challenge to minimize our tax exposure and improve our bottom line or our take-home pay. We then take advice from nonexperts or take chances where we believe opportunities appear to exist to reduce our tax exposure and realize too late that the opportunities do not sustain the scrutiny of the IRS or meet with their approval.

We face the risk of the punitive measures the IRS can implement such as penalties and interest which are not only unpalatable but can result in us not only finding ourselves in serious financial trouble but also facing the risk of criminal prosecution.

Not only is tax a complex subject and the subject of much complicated legislative enactments but it is also the subject of vast case law and expert publications be it in special report or article form. A subject, so complex and involved, that the average businessperson simply does not have the time, understanding, or ability to comprehend all that is set out in the vast literature to actually deal with the tax problems that can beset them! In essence an expert or the establishment of or access to a team of experts in this area is so often a much-needed resource to effectively and promptly handle tax matters on both a business and personal level.

Saving Money in the Wrong Places

VERY OFTEN PEOPLE are reluctant or reticent in approaching tax experts because of the perceived cost involved. We become "penny wise and pound foolish"! We would rather not spend the money up front and run the risk of paying a greater price later. Not a wise course—at times the cost of the right advice not only helps reduce the greater risk of penalties and interest but gives that much-needed peace of mind. What price tag can you attach to that?

So what is the best advice or counsel to take here? When you have a problem or face a potential problem be it in the arena of tax or be it any other arena for that matter, go to the person, the expert who can fix it, or at least advise you on the best course of action, or even assist you in finding a solution. Better still, try and avoid the problem in the first place by applying the "prevention is better than cure" principle. Get the right advice from the experts up front and so avoid problems completely (hopefully) down the line.

There are tax experts out there—use them! It is far wiser and definitely more prudent than trying to do it on your own. If you are in business you can retain such tax experts or consultants on your tax team and use them effectively as and when the need arises. Alternatively, if you are able to, create your own tax team but still have access to the necessary external experts so that you have an outside objective viewpoint. Don't run the risk of being subject to a potentially subjective and even emotive viewpoint, because your own tax team is intimately in the cut and thrust of the problems and internal politics that go hand in hand with them. Sometimes, an outsider is quick to see a problem with a "fresh pair of eyes" than the person who is caught up in the issues and is factory blind or "cannot see the wood for the trees."

In the case of small businesses, in exchange for a small monthly commitment, the tax-Radar™ program is made available through their accountants to offer all the expertise they need.

One plus One Equals Three or Four or More

NOTHING OF SIGNIFICANCE was ever achieved by an individual acting alone. A Chinese proverb states, "Behind an able man there are always other able men." A team working together is always at the heart of great achievement. Doing it alone is less effective.

President Lyndon Johnson, a former president of the United States of America, said, "There are no problems we cannot solve together and very few that we solve by ourselves." Teams involving more people afford more resources, ideas, and energy than an individual. Strengths are maximized and weaknesses exposed and minimized. A team provides multiple perspectives on how to find solutions, be they actual or potential, and thus several alternatives are derived for each problem or situation. Teams simply do more than an individual.

The question is not whether you can do everything yourself, it's how soon you realize that you cannot. Andrew Carnegie said, "It makes a big step in your development when you come to realize that other people can help you do a better job than you could do alone."

Woodrow Wilson, former president of the United States of America, said, "We should not only use all the brains we have, but all those we can borrow."

When people underestimate the difficulty of achieving big things or overcoming difficulties they try to do it alone! Don't learn the truth too late and find yourself in a deeper hole than when you first started. Consultant John Ghegan has a sign on his desk which reads, "If I had to do it all over again, I'd get help!" Don't let that be your experience. Don't try to do it on your own—create a tax team!

> *"In your attempt to overcome the challenges of tax risk management, you will constantly find yourself in a position where you will need assistance from those more knowledgeable than you. In doing so, do not misunderstand or confuse your needs with theirs."*
>
> Source: *48 Laws of Power*

The Case of Professional Consultants

IN THE VERY competitive field of tax consulting an emerging professional practice realized that it had to apply different marketing tactics to differentiate itself from the major attorney and accounting firms that it was trying to compete against. The problem that faced Professional Consultants was the fact that many major corporations had long-standing relationships with these established and large attorney and accounting firms, and their ability to lure these corporations away from the big firms was virtually impossible. It had to devise a new strategy in analyzing the market; it realized that the major accounting firms, selling tax consulting services, had a major disadvantage in the services they offered. Anything they did with their clients would or could be summoned and attached by the IRS in any tax audit. This meant that advice opinions, consultation notes, and tax concerns recorded by the auditing firms could become a major source of highly sensitive information to the IRS, as none of it was subject to legal privilege. Had any corporation shared sensitive concerns with its accountant tax advisors, it ran the real risk that the IRS would have access to this advice and information, exposing the heart of the tax-sensitive problems, before they could get resolved.

Professional Consultants (a multidisciplinary practice including a team of attorneys) realized that big law firms did not traditionally get involved in tax compliance or tax risk management issues, generally dealt with by the accounting firms. Their focus was more in the advice and planning phases of big transactions or direct involvement in the disputes between the IRS and taxpayers. It was uncharacteristic for these law firms to proactively involve themselves in historical, current, and future tax risk management strategies and processes, despite the fact that they could provide legal privilege to taxpayers when sensitive tax issues are investigated.

Professional Consultants realized that their niche market lay in the gap between the large accounting and attorneys firms, where they could provide the missing link, of acting as a legal privilege conduit for the taxpayer in getting their usual technical tax advice without standing on the toes of the big accounting and attorney firms. They would also position themselves to form part of a corporation's legal team in the tax team coordinating and guiding under their supervision any sensitive information flow under the legal privilege umbrella, until the appropriate time for disclosure occurred. In this note, briefs could be issued to the accountants and the attorneys, all tax-sensitive information could be protected by legal privilege, and pre- and post-legal and tax audits could be orchestrated after the conclusion of large transactions.

A win-win formula that provided the taxpayer corporations with legal privilege protection, without treading on the toes of big accounting and law firms. For more information look at www.7taxrisks.com.

The Tax Team

THE TYPICAL TAX team consists of the following personalities:

☐ BO/CFO

☐ tax manager

☐ accounting tax advisors and other outside tax advisors

❏ the legal team, as leaders of the tax team to ensure legal privilege

❏ in the case of a small business, the entire tax team is offered through the tax-Radar™ program, at no additional cost

❏ The various participants in the tax team need to be carefully defined.

BO/CFO or Business Owner

IT IS VERY important that the BO/CFO or business owner (in the case of small businesses) takes a primary role and interest in the tax risk management affairs of the business. It often happens in businesses that the BO/CFO or business owner merely is the point of contact for a tax compliance officer to report to. This has to change in order to ensure that a culture of transparency toward tax risk management issues starts developing in the business. The BO/CFO or business owner will obviously have a very close liaison with the CEO, the audit committee, and other board members from time to time. It is imperative that he or she has a very direct interest in the tax risk management issues being monitored and managed by the tax manager.

The BO/CFO or business owner will become the reporting link to the audit committee and the rest of the board.

Usually the BO/CFO or business owner, as member of the tax team, will be the point of contact with the tax compliance officer, with officials from the IRS and the IRS representative, in the event that it is necessary to make representations to the IRS in respect of any of the tax risk management TRM™ issues under consideration.

The BO/CFO or business owner will be the chairperson of all the tax team meetings that take place from time to time. As the head of financial issues within the business, all tasks emanating from the tax team meetings will ultimately involve reporting directly back to him via the tax compliance officer of the business. In this way transparency and ongoing communication is ensured.

Tax Manager

FROM THE OUTSET it should be made clear that the tax manager role in a small business is usually handled by the accountant. The accountant will now have the comfort of 24/7 support under the tax-Radar™ program offered through the accounting firm of the small business.

Apart from being a skilled tax compliance officer, the tax manager will not only be responsible for usual tax compliance duties but will also be responsible for ensuring that the uncovered tax risk areas within the business are properly dealt with. In order to be able to do this the tax manager must have direct access to the BO/CFO or business owner. In this regard the tax manager must be able to communicate directly with the BO/CFO or the business owner in the event that there are any concerns that the tax manager may have in relation to these transactions.

The tax manager must have access to the internal audit team of the business and as such be entitled to review any financial accounting issues which the tax manager believes may have a tax impact. In this regard there are many historical financial accounting issues relating to accounting provisions, related party transactions, and the like which may have created tax risk issues, which tax risk issues have not been uncovered in the past, simply because they have not been thoroughly examined. Open access must be given to the tax manager to attend to these functions and duties.

The tax manager must have access to the heads of operations to be able to communicate with them and to review any operational transactions that they may become involved in, once again to assess any emerging tax risks that may occur as a result of steps taken in these operating divisions or subsidiaries.

The tax manager is responsible for driving the tax strategy process within the business and in this regard is responsible for ensuring that a date, time, and place is set for the tax strategy process. In addition to this the tax manager is also responsible for ensuring that the tax strategy process be revisited once every six months. In this regard the backing of the BO/CFO or the business owner of the business must be sought and obtained.

The tax manager must organize the tax team meetings, tax reviews, and any of the tax work that flows from the tax team process toward minimizing the tax risk issues within the business.

The tax manager will form the point of contact between the business and the IRS representative who will be met with from time to time to ensure that the tax risk issues that are being reviewed within the business are brought up to date and communicated, where need be, with the IRS.

Accounting and Other Outside Tax Advisors

ACCOUNTING AND OTHER outside tax advisors will form a very important part of the tax team. In the case of a small business this component is taken care of through the tax-Radar™ program.

They will be requested to review all historical and current tax information relating to the businesses that are in their possession. In this regard they will be required to make this information available on a systematic basis to the tax team from time to time in order for the tax team to review this information. The relevance of reviewing the information which is in the possession of these outside tax advisors is to establish what information they have is relevant and irrelevant to any future IRS audit that might be conducted. It should be borne in mind that information which is in the possession of these outside tax advisors which may be irrelevant may in any event be attached by the IRS officials conducting audits, which in turn may lead to unnecessary avenues being explored by the IRS officials giving rise to additional resources having to be allocated in an attempt to show the IRS officials that the information is irrelevant. In practice what normally happens is that this irrelevant information leads to a whole host of unnecessary questions and investigations which ends up wasting everybody's time.

These outside tax advisors will also be key in participating in giving the historical perspective to any potential tax issues or problems that have been identified within the tax team. In this regard these historical perspectives will play a very important role in determining which of the potential tax issues should fall on-the-radar screen and which of these should fall off-the-radar screen. Often participants from the outside tax advisors have been involved with the business for a very long time and are able to give very in-depth information as to the reasons behind certain transactions having taken place in the past.

The Legal Team

> "These best practices include: (1) communicating clearly with the client regarding the terms of the engagement and the form and scope of the advice or assistance to be rendered; (2) establishing the relevant acts, including evaluating the reasonableness of any assumptions or representations; (3) relating applicable law, including potentially applicable judicial doctrines, to the relevant facts; (4) arriving at a conclusion supported by the law and the facts; (5) advising the client regarding the import of the conclusions reached; and (6) acting fairly and with integrity in practice before the IRS."
>
> Source: Regulations Governing Practice Before the IRS,
> Practice Before the IRS, Section 10,33

THE LEGAL TEAM must have experience in the tax risk management TRM™ process that is being embarked upon by the business, involving a multiskilled group of participants who must play different roles in the review of the on-the-radar screen and off-the-radar screen tax issues. The legal team function will be fully covered in the tax-Radar™ program offered to the small business through its accounting firm.

The legal team must also be tasked with the responsibility of holding all sensitive information flowing from the tax team tax risk management process so that this sensitive tax information can be reviewed and analyzed before the outcomes are discussed with the other members of the tax team, the audit committee, and finally the board. It is ultimately the decision of the board then what to do with the outcome that flows from this sensitive information in the hands of the legal team, subject to legal privilege.

They will be involved in collating, requesting, and distributing any technical opinions sought from outside tax advisors to ensure the legal privilege at all times over these opinions. Where necessary, they will attach any supporting documentation which has been obtained by a factual analysis of the facts surrounding or giving rise to these opinions being sought, which supporting facts, as attached to these opinions, will also fall under this legal privilege. This will ensure that this information will form part of the opinions, subject to the legal privilege, and will tie down all loose ends that may create problems for the business going forward, being tied down in a structured and logical sequence and format.

Chapter 3

Direction? Compile a TRM™ Strategy

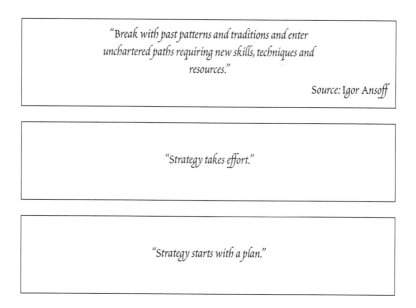

> "Break with past patterns and traditions and enter
> unchartered paths requiring new skills, techniques and
> resources."
>
> Source: Igor Ansoff

> "Strategy takes effort."

> "Strategy starts with a plan."

Executive Summary

ANY BUSINESS GOAL that is set without a carefully thought out and planned strategy will often end in failure. It is a common problem in many businesses that the people involved in tax compliance, other than in the area of traditional tax compliance, don't know what to do when they encounter a problem. As a result a tax team should be assembled to create cohesion and communication in the process of devising a set tax risk management TRM™ strategy.

It is simple enough to devise a strategy that will provide the direction. However, there is no quick remedy; a proper process must be put in place. Of importance for this process, and the information divulged in this process, to be subject to legal privilege.

The basic strategy is for the organization to undergo a SWOT (strengths, weaknesses, opportunities, and threats) analysis from a tax point of view. Focus primarily on the weaknesses and threats; this is the area where the majority of your liability will lie. Two broad types of issues must be identified: those on-the-radar screen and those off-the-radar screen.

These risks that are on-the-radar screen are those that are known to the organization as well as the IRS. They are issues that are ongoing and that have some history behind them. However, a strategy of how to deal with these problems must be established, and a strategy must be developed in order to limit the risk of these problem areas. For instance, a tax manager may be aware that the IRS has raised a significant assessment in respect of outstanding VAT. It may be apparent that there is real risk of a liability; and in an effort to clear the problem as quickly as possible the taxpayer pays the full amount of the assessment, including interest and penalties, without looking at other aspects of the assessment raised by the IRS, such as the procedure employed by the IRS in raising the assessment, or entering into negotiations to reduce the amount of interest and penalties.

The off-the-radar screen risks are those risks that the business is aware of and has noted but has not done anything about them. That is to say that the IRS has no clue of the existence of these tax risks. The strategy in this instance must be clear and effective. All the risks must be identified and prioritized. Bear in mind that once the business has started dealing with these various risks, it is important that the IRS be involved at the appropriate point of time in the future to minimize the cost of compliance through a carefully implemented plan of self-disclosure to them, averting penalties and some interest. If no disclosure to them is required, the matters are simply filed away, where accessible, with all the facts and opinions intact.

Don't forget the strengths and opportunities that have been identified. On the positive side of tax risk management a business can look at its effective tax rate in comparison with other similar businesses and determine whether it is paying more or less tax in its country of origin or abroad.

If the tax paid is significantly higher then something needs to be done! Start by scrutinizing the expenditure and allowance for assets to ensure that you can take advantage of any benefits allowed by legislation.

Introduction

IN CHAPTER 1 the necessity for proactive tax risk management was discussed. In chapter 2 the need to create a participating tax team was explained. Following on from this, this chapter deals with TRM™ Step 3.

Most businesses do not have a road map of how and where they are going with their tax risk management, other than blindly ensuring that they are "fully tax compliant." Without a properly formulated TRM™ strategy in place, the goals and objectives, and the manner of executing a TRM™ process so as to minimize tax risk, cannot be achieved properly. An extensive, and fully maintained, TRM™ strategy is what is required.

In the case of small businesses that participate in the tax-Radar™ program, the tax strategy component is taken care of through the completion of the Tax Risk Matrix with their accounting firm and any tax risk issues that may arise will be dealt with in accordance with the tax-Radar™ mandate between the parties.

Knowledge, Strategy, and Communication

THE MAJORITY OF business decisions you will make will have some kind of tax implication. Knowledge and understanding is the key in managing your tax liability. So what does this involve? By now, you have created a tax team around you. This tax team needs to develop a tax strategy with clear goals in order to direct the business in the most efficient tax manner. Understand that developing a tax strategy does not mean avoiding taxation. Rather it is a means of identifying where the tax risks lie. Without a clear tax strategy that everyone is aware of, miscommunication will result.

SWOT Analysis

TO GET A better understanding, in all businesses there will be decisions that have been made in the past, decisions currently being made, and decisions that will need to be made in the future. These decisions must be carefully analyzed and certain tax risk exposure areas must be identified and prioritized in each respect. In order to develop such a strategy, a SWOT (strengths, weaknesses, opportunities, and threats) analysis must be conducted. The business should firstly focus on the threats and weaknesses and then take a look at the strengths and opportunities.

It is important to identify the different areas where the risk lies. Your team will undertake to look at all aspects of the business. Start off by looking at the current risk exposure. The obvious starting point would be to assess anything that is currently "on-the-radar screen."

For example: Are there any audits under way? Are there any investigations into any aspects of the business? Are there any outstanding queries with the IRS? These will all be matters that revenue will be aware of. Then you must go further; take a look at your records and compile the information that you gather. In all likelihood there will be other aspects that revenue has not picked up on where you may lie exposed.

Once the current standing of the business has been assessed, take a look at risks that are off-the-radar screen. Off-the-radar screen activities are of particular importance here, i.e., activities that were never picked up by the IRS or the business for that matter. Make a note of risks or possible risks that are concerning. They will also include risks that the business is aware of but where nothing has been done about it. These risks must be assessed and prioritized with a clear strategy developed for each risk area. The risks must also be prioritized with the most pressing risk being dealt with as urgently as possible.

Don't forget the strengths and opportunities that have been identified. On the positive side of tax risk management a business can look at its effective tax rate in comparison to other similar businesses and determine whether it is paying more or less the same tax in the country of origin. If the tax paid is significantly higher then something needs to be done! Start by scrutinizing the expenditure and allowance for assets to ensure that you can take advantage of any benefits allowed to them by legislation.

The TRM™ Strategy Plan

THE INCREASING SIGNIFICANCE of measuring and managing tax risk in any taxpaying corporation is underpinned by the introduction of SOX 404 (Sarbanes-Oxley Act of 2002 in the USA, Section 404) and now FIN 48 (Financial Accounting Standards Board Interpretation No. 48, "Accounting for Uncertainty for Income Taxes") issued by the Financial Accounting Standards Board in the United States of America. Both these developments emphasize the importance of transparent corporate governance.

Many material discrepancies in corporations relate specifically to tax risk management problems.

Independent surveys conducted on SOX 404 have shown that on average 30% of the material discrepancy filings to the SEC (United States Securities Exchange Commission) are **tax-related problems**.

Tax risk is one of the risk areas within a business that is difficult to quantify and manage unless a significant tax risk management TRM™ process has been effected in that organization. Many of the tax risks have nothing to do with the current financial year and in many instances relate to prior financial periods which may go back many years. What is more is that research has shown that the tax risks exposed do not just reside in the area of tax compliance but emanate from the areas of financial accounting, transactions, and the operations of the corporation.

The TRM™ process also relies on the input of key tax technical advisors in each of those jurisdictions to assist in making an effective determination as to the extent of the tax risk issue. Once that has been determined the most appropriate advice and recommendations can be made to senior management in the corporation as to the practical way forward to manage and resolve the tax risk.

"Determine the key factors of success (KFS)."

Source: Kenichi Ohmae

"10 Principles of Success

1. *Learn to fight;*
2. *Do it right;*
3. *Expect the worst;*
4. *Burn the bridges;*
5. *Pull together;*
6. *Show me the way;*
7. *Know the facts;*
8. *Seize the day;*
9. *Do it better;*
10. *Keep them guessing."*

Source: Sun Tzu

The overall big picture TRM™ strategy is illustrated diagrammatically as follows:

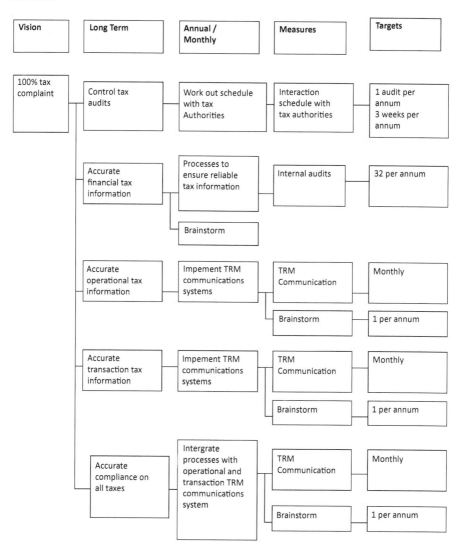

The Root Causes of Tax Risk

THE MOST LIKELY cause is an unyielding appetite of the government for tax, a bad relationship with the IRS, and tax compliance shortcomings through unreliable and unaudited source material that introduces the material weakness of an additional unpredictable tax exposure.

All taxes will yield mistakes made in the financial reporting, transactions, and operations areas of a business.

One of the best methods for exposing the tax unreliability in the tax compliance, transactions, financial reporting, and operations divisions is through brainstorming sessions involving the appointed tax team. In the case of small businesses, this is done through completion of the Tax Risk Matrix as part of the tax-Radar™ program.

"3 MAJOR Myths

1. Successful corporates maximize profits first and foremost!

   NO—Visionary corporates pursue a cluster of objectives; money is only one; core values and a sense of PURPOSE is the biggest.

2. Big corporations play it safe!

   NO—They're not afraid to set BHAGs (Big Hairy Audacious Goals). Daunting and risky goals to challenge its people!

3. Highly successful companies make their best moves by brilliant/complex strategic planning.

   NO—Often their brilliance is by sheer accident through trial and error. Try lots of stuff keep what works."

Source: Built to Last by Collins and Porras

In a recent tax survey conducted on the Internet and distributed to tax professionals via the Web site www.7taxrisks.com the identified root causes of tax risk can be summarized as follows:

❑ Only 15% of the survey participants are certain they are 100% tax compliant.

❑ Seventy-nine percent have no tax strategy.

❑ Between 50 and 60% do not have at least monthly communication with the transactions and operations divisions in their businesses.

❑ Forty percent do not have their tax returns up to date.

❑ Sixty percent to 80% have not had IRS-related tax audits in the last two years.

❑ Only 16% of the boards of directors discuss tax strategy and tax planning at their board meetings.

Prevent the Problem

THIS SECTION FOCUSES on the countermeasures required to reduce or eliminate the root causes.

The problem is the unpredictable nature of tax in the taxpayer, especially as the tax authorities become increasingly more vigilant and aggressive in pursuing dishonest taxpayers.

The root cause is the insatiable appetite of the State to increase its ability to collect taxes to fund increasing State expenditure, the perception that taxpayers underpay taxes, and the calculated guess that only about 40% of tax risk is usually attended to by the tax compliance divisions of taxpayers. The other 60% tax risk resides in the transactions, operations, and financial divisions of the taxpayer.

The root causes can be summarized as follows, with potential countermeasures:

❑ The insatiable appetite of the State for money:

○ Countermeasure 1—State lobbying.

○ Countermeasure 2—Vote for a new government.

○ Countermeasure 3—Move the business to another jurisdiction.

❑ IRS negative perception:

○ Countermeasure 1—Build relationship with IRS representative.

○ Countermeasure 2—Call for on-the-radar screen issues with a plan to resolve these.

○ Countermeasure 3—Ensure timely returns, fair provisional tax payments, and meeting positively the key indicators set by the tax authorities as to compliancy levels.

Tax compliance division shortcomings with unreliable information (which requires countermeasures for each of the supporting financial, operations, and transactions divisions):

○ Financial countermeasures

■ Countermeasure 1—Ensure "tamper proof" transfer of accounting information to the tax return supporting annexures.

■ Countermeasure 2—Regular internal tax audits in the various key tax areas (sales tax, VAT, payroll taxes, income tax, customs, and excise), with external consultant supervision.

■ Countermeasure 3—Analysis of all old accounting provisions, especially those loaded onto a SAP or Oracle database systems, where old records are not available.

○ Operations countermeasures

■ Countermeasure 1—Regular e-mail, meeting, and other communication between operations and tax compliance.

■ Countermeasure 2—Tax training and awareness of various transactions and potential tax implications.

■ Countermeasure 3—Regular internal audits to review what is reported as being subject to tax provisions.

○ Transactions countermeasures

- Countermeasure 1—Regular communication between operations and tax compliance.

- Countermeasure 2—Tax training and awareness of various transactions and potential tax implications.

- Countermeasure 3—Legal and tax audits of key major transactions over the last ten years to ensure proper compliance with planning of transactions, proper implementation, and postimplementation processes.

Sun Tzu on Strategy

- *There is no constant, victory is through endless adaptation.*

- *On information, know the conditions of opponents.*

- *On tactics, turn problems into advantages.*

- *On competition, know the plans of your competitors to make informed alliances.*

- *On leadership and people management, those who do not submit are hard to employ.*

- *On communication, issue directives consistently.*

Through the tax-Radar™ program smaller businesses will be informed regularly of the position of the IRS toward their business (if announced) and will receive regular directives of what needs to be done to minimize known tax risks that are being targeted by the IRS.

Communication

IN THE PROCESS of implementing the tax risk management TRM™ system, in order to minimize tax risk on an ongoing basis, it will be necessary to implement a communication system between the tax compliance division, the financial accounting divisions, the transaction division, and the operations of the corporation. The communication process will require frequent documentation which attempts to highlight any tax risk that has developed in each of the mentioned divisions to the tax compliance division, through a systematic series of questionnaires generated by the tax compliance division. This will ensure that the tax manager is able to connect with key areas in the business to get a firsthand account of what is happening in "real time," rather than waiting for financial accounting feedback in six months' time.

Many of the problems around tax risk that are hidden in a business result from the lack of communication between the tax manager, who is responsible for tax compliance, and the key personnel involved in transactions, financial accounting, and operations. Words speak louder than mere numbers in this case.

This process is discussed in greater detail in chapter 7 of this special report.

Methodology

AN EXPERIENCED FIRM that will manage the TRM™ strategies must be well positioned to take the methodology to the various divisions in the business. In doing so, the TRM™ firm must not necessarily be tax specialists but must work very closely with associated technical tax firms through an established network, who have the required expertise to assist in giving opinions in those tax risk areas that require attention. The TRM™ management firm must facilitate the whole process from inception to completion. They act as the external project champion with the key business role players in the tax team. They will review the law, the facts, and the conclusions so as to test the viability and quality of the technical advice against the actual position that the business finds itself in, with the guidance of technical tax specialists in the appropriate jurisdiction. This methodology has worked very well for multinationals in TRM™ projects in the past.

In providing the tax risk management TRM™ service the required tax technical assistance will be obtained from the tax services and litigation support services of various carefully selected independent tax advisors and specialists.

This service is offered comprehensively through the tax-Radar™ program to smaller businesses.

Machiavelli on Strategy

- *Successful leadership requires skill and shrewdness.*
- *Train loyalty to ensure employees get things done in a highly predictable manner.*

Hamel on Strategy

- *Strategy is a calendar-driven ritual involving plans and subplans.*
- *Great strategies come from challenging the status quo and doing something different.*
- *Strategy needs to be freed from the tyranny of senior management.*
- *People embrace change if given some control over their own future.*
- *Strategy must be democratic.*
- *Anyone can be a strategy activist.*
- *Gain a new perspective, look for new potential markets through new eyes.*
- *Create unpredictable outcomes, and let go.*
- *Strategy innovation is the only way to succeed in the face of any enormous resource disadvantages.*

Source: Igor Ansoff

The Pretax Strategy Preparation

A GOOD STARTING point in preparing for the TRM™ strategy process is for the BO/CFO, together with the tax manager, to complete the following TRM™ best practice checklist prepared by PricewaterhouseCoopers in their tax risk management guide.

Best Practice Tax Risk Checklist

Figure 1: Best practice checklist

Internal Control Component	Question	Yes	No
Control environment	Do you have a documented tax risk management policy?		
	Are there specific tax risk management objectives?		
	Have all relevant stakeholders had input to the policy?		
	Have all the tax risk areas been included?		
	Has the tax risk management policy been discussed and agreed at board level?		
	Has the policy and objectives been communicated to all stakeholders?		
	Is there an appetite in the business to implement the policy?		
	Does the board review the position at least once a year?		
	Is the tax risk management policy aligned with the wider objectives of the business?		
Risk assessment	Are there procedures in place to assess the tax risks in the business?		
	Do they cover all areas of tax risk?		
	Do they cover all taxes?		
	Do they cover all significant countries in the group?		
	Do you know who are the key creators of tax risk in your organization?		
	Do you have process in place to manage these people?		
	Do you know what the five key tax risks are in the business?		
	Do you use scenario planning to assess risk?		
	Are tax risks considered in aggregate to allow an overall portfolio view of risks to be considered?		
	Is the tax risk assessment documented?		
Control activities	Are risk control procedures in place?		
	Are the five key tax risks in the business being properly managed?		
	Is it clear to the business when they need to consult the tax function?		

	Is it clear when the tax function needs to consult with the board?		
	Are control activities communicated and embedded throughout the organization?		
	Is it clear who in the organization has responsibility for individual control activities?		
	Are the detailed control activities documented agreed at board level?		
	Are you properly supporting those who have a risk mitigation role (e.g., the shadow tax function)?		
Information and Communication	Is the board kept aware of the key tax risks in the business?		
	Is the board consulted on major tax risk matters?		
	Is there a central place people can find out about the business's tax risk policy?		
	Is there a list of people (or roles) who need to understand their role within tax risk management?		
	Are people new to roles within tax risk management briefed on tax risk management as it affects them?		
	Is the shadow tax department briefed on tax risk management?		
	Is there training in place to ensure key individuals understand their role in tax risk management?		
	Are processes in place to ensure the tax function is kept aware of operational changes to the business?		
Monitoring	Is there a process in place to ensure that tax risk management control activities are operating effectively?		
	Are internal audit involved?		
	Are the results of monitoring activities reported back to senior management?		
	Is the monitoring process documented?		
	Is remedial action taken where risk assessment and control activities are not found to be operating effectively?		

Source: Tax Risk Management Guide, PWC,
www.pwc.com/extweb/pwcpublications.nsf/docid/cee8da1dd856bea780256e97003d6898

A Tax Risk Management Survey

WHAT FOLLOWS IS an example of a report generated from a tax risk survey conducted on www.7taxrisks.com which takes into account the answers to certain key questions and then analyzes the effect that those answers have on the overall undisclosed tax risk that the business may be facing. This can be combined with figure 1 and figure 5 below to create a more comprehensive analysis of potential undisclosed tax risk areas in a business:

Figure 2: Summary comments on seven TRM™ steps survey

Question	Question Detail	Answer	Comments	Concerns	Cumulative Uncovered Tax Risk
#1	VAT Returns	Yes			
#2	Document rating	Good	All documentary evidence must be rated as excellent for accuracy and availability.	Any rating less than excellent increases IRS audit risk. Your document archiving system should be carefully checked, with ongoing spot checks.	10% of uncovered tax risk exposure.
#3	Provisional tax	Yes			
#4	Provisional tax 20% variance	No			
#5	IT returns	Yes			

Question	Question Detail	Answer	Comments	Concerns	Cumulative Uncovered Tax Risk
#6	IRS queries	Yes	Great care must be taken in the manner in which these queries are answered. See #7 below.		
#7	IRS audit	No	IRS would like to audit all businesses every five years, and do audits more frequently. An audit can be expected in the near future. The fact that there are outstanding queries means that an audit may follow. Great care must be taken in the manner in which these queries are answered.	Internal tax audits must be performed to ensure unambiguous tax opinions are in place and that all tax records and transactions are accurate, failing which additional tax penalties and interest, together with uncovered taxes will result at the conclusion of the audit.	20% of uncovered tax risk exposure.
#8	Internal audit	No	This is a great concern as there will definitely be a number of tax exposures that need to be uncovered.	To minimize tax risk, at the very least, there should be an internal audit process that takes place every twelve months to limit uncovered tax risk exposure.	30% of uncovered tax risk exposure.

Question	Question Detail	Answer	Comments	Concerns	Cumulative Uncovered Tax Risk
#9 and #10	Compliance officer communicates	No No	Shows lack of internal communication with operating divisions, one of the main causes of 60% uncovered tax risks in many businesses.	This will give rise to uncovered tax risk in the areas of financial accounting, transactions, and operations, adding 10% to your uncovered tax risk exposure.	40% of uncovered tax risk exposure.
#11	Mergers, etc.	Yes	All transactions, unless very carefully documented, and given opinion on, with fully available documentation, having been subjected to a recent tax and legal audit, will give rise to uncovered tax risk that may be sizeable, depending upon how large the transactions were.	The lack of appropriate opinions and the failure to have conducted a recent tax and legal audit on large transactions will increase the uncovered tax risk.	50% of uncovered tax risk exposure.

Question	Question Detail	Answer	Comments	Concerns	Cumulative Uncovered Tax Risk
#12	Stock provisions	No	Provisions, with the implementation of a SAP system (see #13 below), will give rise to significant uncovered tax risks, especially where an internal tax audit on these tax provisions has not been performed historically.	This gives rise to heightened uncovered tax risk for financial accounting and specifically historical provisions around the time that SAP was implemented.	
#13	SAP	Yes	Refer to #12 above.		
#14	Six Sigma	No	This shows careful attention is probably NOT paid to various deficiencies in the business.	Ensure there is also a tax risk management TRM™ Strategy in place.	60% of uncovered tax risk exposure.

Question	Question Detail	Answer	Comments	Concerns	Cumulative Uncovered Tax Risk
#15	Offshore	Yes Sub-sidiary	Many businesses failing to keep accurate policies in place that match the treatment of transactions in later years of assessment. Incorrect advice, ignoring the subjective nature of the relationship between parent and subsidiary may also have led to unnecessary uncovered tax risk exposure. Merely following the arm's length approach set out in benchmark studies such as *Amadeus* may also prove to be problematical.	Failure to keep annual up-to-date policies filed with the IRS in line with actual practice in the business may lead to unnecessary penalties and interest on any transfer pricing exposure.	70% of uncovered tax risk exposure.

Source: *www.7taxrisks.com*

Figure 3: Uncovered tax risk

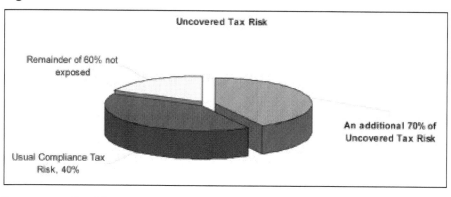

Source: *www.7taxrisks.com*

Figure 3 shows what a tax compliance department traditionally covers in tax risk management, approximately 40% of the overall tax risk of the business. Another 60% uncovered tax risk potentially remains.

After doing the tax risk survey, of the potential uncovered tax risk exposure of 60%, the results show that the business in figure 2 may have an additional 70% uncovered tax exposure. These are not accurate results but an indicator that the business has potential major uncovered tax risks.

In practical terms, if the business were to pay PAYE, payroll taxes, sales tax, VAT, and income tax of $1m per year, it is possible that on the completion of a successful IRS audit, an additional $1.05m may be exposed.

The IRS could go back ten years, add up to 75% penalties and interest, which would double the outstanding taxes payable.

This means that all the IRS have to uncover over that ten-year period is unpaid taxes of only $17,500 per year.

One hundred seventy-five thousand dollars for the ten years.

Plus 75% penalties takes the sum to $306,250.

Plus interest, which over ten years will double, the additional uncovered tax amount increases to over $600,000.

The solutions lie in overcoming the seven TRM™ steps through

❑ proactive tax risk management as set out in this special report;

❑ having a tax team present through the tax-radar program;

❑ compiling a tax risk management TRM™ strategy through completion of the Tax Risk Matrix;

❑ overcoming insular tax compliance through educational communication in the tax-radar program;

❑ remedying defective financial accounting through ongoing maintenance of the Tax Risk Matrix;

❑ facts, facts, and more facts to overcome defective transactions through interactive communication in the tax-radar program; and

❑ implementing effective communication with operations with webinar, www.tax-Radar.com, and other forms of ongoing communication.

Types of Tax Risk

THE FOLLOWING TYPICAL events will help to determine the types of tax risk that may be found in the business.

Figure 4: Types of tax risk

Type of tax risk	Typical events giving rise to tax risk
Transactional	Acquisitions
	Disposals
	Mergers
	Financing transactions
	Tax-driven cross-border transactions
	Internal reorganizations
	Stock options
Operational	New business ventures
	New operating models
	Operating in new locations
	New operating structures (e.g., JVs or partnerships)
	Commenced new technological developments (e.g., Internet trading)
	Lack of communication
Compliance	Lack of proper management
	Weak accounting records or controls
	Data integrity issues
	Insufficient resources
	Systems changes in last three years
	Revenue investigations in last three years
	What is your document archive rating?
	Are all your tax returns up to date and submitted?
	Do you operate offshore?
	Subsidiaries
Financial accounting	Changes in legislation
	Changes in accounting systems
	Changes in accounting policies and GAAP

Management	Changes in personnel—both in tax and in the business
	Experienced tax people leaving—and information being in their heads and not properly documented
	New and inexperienced resources
Reputational	IRS raid or investigation
	Press comment
	Court hearings and legal actions
	Political developments

Source: Tax Risk Management Guide, PWC, adapted by the author, www.pwc.com/extweb/pwcpublications.nsf/docid/cee8da1dd856bea780256e97003d6898

Quantify the Tax Risk

PART OF THE tax strategy process is to quantify the potential tax risk which will assist in illustrating the cost to the business of its tax risk exposure. The table below designed by PricewaterhouseCoopers in their tax risk management guide contains some examples to illustrate the point.

Figure 5: Quantify the potential tax risk

Event	Chance of tax risk event happening %A	Impact $'m B	Potential cost $'m A X B
Acquisitions	75	10	7.5
Disposals	25	40	10.0
Mergers	10	20	2.0
Financing transactions	60	5	3.0
Tax-driven transactions	20	5	1.0
Internal reorganizations	5	10	0.5
New business ventures	20	5	1.0
New operating models	50	8	4.0
Operating in new locations	25	2	0.5
New operating structures	20	3	0.6
Impact of technological developments (e.g., Internet trading)	80	5	4.0

Lack of proper management	4	The previous years of tax liability, divided by 40, multiplied by 60 stated as a $ value. For example, $40m/40 X 60 = $60m	4% of $60m in the example = $2,4m
Weak accounting records or controls	4		
Data integrity issues	4		
Insufficient resources	12		
Systems changes	4		
Legislative changes	12		
Revenue investigations	12		
Changes in accounting systems	4		
Changes in accounting policy and GAAP	4		
Changes in personnel—both in tax and in the business	4		
Experienced people leaving	4		
Inexperienced resources	4		
Revenue authority raid or investigation	16		
Press comment	4		
Court hearing/legal action	4		
Political developments	4		
Total Tax Risk	-	-	$34.1m

Source: Tax Risk Management Guide, PWC, adapted by the author, www.pwc.com/extweb/pwcpublications.nsf/docid/cee8da1dd856bea780256e97003d6898

Figure 5 and figure 2 could be combined to create a more thorough tax risk assessment and quantification in a business, so as to illustrate to the audit committee and to the board the potential tax risk that a business may be facing. The criteria and the weighting for each business will have to be carefully determined, so as not to create distortions that fly in the face of a realistic projection. At best, the calculations at this stage of the process will be an educated guesstimate. The quantification becomes more accurate as the opinion sign-off stage is completed.

Set the Tax Risk Management TRM™ Strategy Process and Project Plan

THE INITIAL PLANNING process is facilitated by the TRM™ facilitator in conjunction with the BO/CFO, financial manager, and tax manager. It entails

❑ appointing the tax risk management TRM™ strategy participants,

❑ planning the tax risk management TRM™ strategy session,

❑ setting the specific tax risk objectives,

❑ planning the tax risk reduction strategy,

❑ planning the factual gathering process,

❑ planning the analytical and solutions process,

❑ determining the closure date, and

❑ setting the parameters for the future maintenance process.

❑ During this defining process, the BO/CFO will be able to identify and validate the process that will reduce the tax risk of the business, illustrate the business processes to be implemented, define the requirements to minimize tax risks, and satisfy the IRS. Make the appropriate preparations to be an effective project leader.

Appointing the Tax Risk Management TRM™ Strategy Participants

This entails

❑ appointing the tax team; and

❑ forming the tax steering committee.

The tax team appointment process has been dealt with in chapter 2 above.

The tax team will report to the tax steering committee. The tax steering committee will report to the audit committee. Tax team meetings will take place frequently. Tax steering committee meetings will take place monthly.

Determine a Tax Team Charter

IT MAY BE useful to determine a tax team charter, which defines the elements of an effective tax team, evaluates the effectiveness of the tax team, determines the guidelines for planning meetings properly and ascertaining effective milestones. Use elements of the Six Sigma process in an adapted form.

The following Six Sigma processes can be adopted for the tax risk management TRM™ strategy process and may prove to be useful in the strategy process:

❑ Quality Function Deployment (QFD) where the tax team can more effectively focus on the activities that will reduce tax risk the most and satisfy the IRS that the business is fully tax compliant, averting unnecessary tax audits and redirecting valuable resources to pursuing the mission of the business, rather than crisis managing tax disputes.

❑ The Cause and Effect Matrix, allowing the tax team to select, prioritize, and analyze the facts collected during the TRM™ process so as to identify the problems in the business that are causing tax risk or that may cause tax risk.

❑ Failure Modes and Effects analysis, helping the tax team to identify and address weaknesses in the tax compliance process before they occur, developing preventative measures targeted at preventing various failure scenarios. This creates total reliability in the tax risk management TRM™ process.

❑ Design of Experiments (DOE) being a statistical technique that includes planning, facts, analysis, and interpretation to determine the relationship between factors affecting a process and the output of that process. The special report is dedicated to the formal TRM™

process designed to plan, obtain the facts, analyze, and interpret the results so that a taxpayer can ultimately determine the relationship between factors affecting the process, such as lack of proactivity, the noninvolvement of a tax team, miscommunication, not obtaining sufficient facts, being too insular, and the effect these have on minimizing tax risk.

These are all useful tools to maximize information while minimizing resources, best implemented through the tax risk management TRM™ strategy process.

Plan to Get Key Facts Out of the Tax Risk Management TRM™ Strategy Session

❑ Assess what tax risk management TRM™ processes currently exist.

❑ What ongoing queries exist with the IRS (on-the-radar screen tax issues)?

❑ What ongoing tax disputes exist with the IRS?

❑ Determine any potential tax risks in the table below (off-the-radar screen issues).

❑ Quantify any potential tax risks exposures by determining the potential risk to the business and the potential costs.

❑ Determine what must be done to reduce tax risk to eliminate conflict with the IRS.

The Tax Risk Reduction Strategy

THE TAX RISKS identified can be reduced, according to a tax risk management guide published by PricewaterhouseCoopers, as follows:

Figure 6: Tax risk reduction strategies

Avoidance	Taking alternative actions so that the risk no longer arises, for example by using a different model such as
	using arm's length transfer price to avoid a transfer pricing tax risk,
	restructuring an asset disposal to be a sale of a shareholding in a company owning those same assets, and
	operating through a legal entity with a different taxable status in a particular location.
Sharing	Taking action to reduce the likelihood or impact of the risk by transferring or sharing the risk in some way. This is generally achieved through the techniques such as the obtaining of warranties or indemnities, obtaining professional opinions, or outsourcing of tax functions.
Reduction	Taking action to reduce the likelihood of the occurrences and/or the impact of the risk, for example by
	interacting within the IRS to cooperate in working through the on-the-radar screen issues;
	carrying out appropriate tax planning;
	obtaining documentary evidence or opinions in support of the proposed tax treatments such as a tax valuation;
	restructuring the event to give a more favorable tax treatment, e.g., by leasing rather than buying a capital asset; and
	carrying out a detailed review of potentially disallowable expenditure to ensure all potentially allowable amounts have been identified and claimed.

Source: Tax Risk Management Guide, PWC,
www.pwc.com/extweb/pwcpublications.nsf/docid/cee8da1dd856bea780256e97003d6898

Plan the Factual Gathering Process

TAKE EACH ON-the-radar screen and off-the-radar screen tax risk identified and create a unique file number, file (hard copy and electronic [pdf] copy), and start assembling all correspondence, documents, notes, agreements, opinions, memoranda, and any other relevant information into date order.

Priorities will differ on a case-by-case basis. The factual gathering process is dealt with in more detail in chapter 5 of this special report.

Plan the Analytical and Solutions Process

THE TAX TECHNICIANS who will assess the tax risk of each on-the-radar screen and off-the-radar screen tax risk issue will be determined, to assist in advising how each tax risk issue must be dealt with now and in the future.

Should any real exposures be identified the conclusions will be submitted, with the appropriate advice obtained via the tax team to the audit committee for final decision.

Determine the Closure Date

A CLOSURE DATE for the tax risk management process is important. Setting open-ended goals will defocus the participants.

The closure date may, however, change, depending upon the outcomes of some of the tax risk issues.

Set the Parameters of the Future Maintenance Process

THIS WILL BE driven by the nature of the tax risk issues dealt with in the tax risk management process.

The TRM™ communication system will also be implemented to ensure effective communication. This is dealt with in greater detail under chapter 7 of this special report.

"The essence in strategy lies in what not to do."

Source: M. Porter

> "*Procrastination can be caused by excessive planning … Paralysis by analysis.*"
>
> Source: *Igor Ansoff*

ABS Ltd. Case Study Report Generated after the Tax Risk Management TRM™ Strategy Workshop

Background

ABS LTD. HAS exposure on tax in numerous areas. Tax issues have been identified as significant with an estimated worst-case exposure in excess of $300m (determined after assessing and quantifying the tax risk in the areas set out below) and if not speedily rectified will have both financial and reputational implications for ABS Ltd.

It is clear that the following key **tax risk** areas exist:

❑ transactional risk

❑ operational risk

❑ compliance risk

❑ financial accounting risk

❑ management risk

❑ reputational risk

High-Level Objectives

The **primary objectives** of the project are as follows:

1. Immediately intercede with the IRS to take control of the process to resolve all tax issues and ensuring the development of an effective working relationship.

2. Conduct a full review of all areas of exposure of ABS Ltd. regarding tax risk, with the end output clarifying the probability of risks and the likelihood of occurrence and the impact on both financial and reputation areas of the exposure materializing.

3. Make recommendations to the audit committee of a plan to resolve these areas of exposure.

4. Ensure that a full and comprehensive plan is prepared for each risk item, irrespective of whether the audit committee decides to address them or not.

5. Following the tax steering committee recommendation, interacting with the IRS to ensure full and final settlement of the risks agreed upon.

The **secondary objectives** are as follows:

1. Ensure the establishment of an effective working relationship between the IRS and ABS Ltd.

2. Set up an effective and appropriate world-class tax department at ABS Ltd. under an appropriately selected tax manager.

3. Ensure that any tax issues arising at the ABS Ltd.'s SA are dealt with in this project period, as far as practically possible.

4. Review the appropriateness of the current accounting firm and tax advisors and recommend changes to the relationships and firms, if necessary.

Tax Team

BO/CFO, Tax Manager, Legal Team, and Existing Tax Advisors.

High-Level Process

	Indicative Timing
Project Commencement	Early June
• Project brief agreed	
• **Tax team** constituted	
Internal Processes	
Information gathering	June-July
Propose high-level process and early interaction with the IRS	End July
Evaluation of risks including follow-up investigations	July-August
Tax team meeting to evaluate risks and agree plan	End August
The IRS Interaction	
Work teams with the IRS	July-February
Tax findings meetings	October-February
Prepare reasons	October-February
Detailed IRS presentations	October-February
Assessments issued / Deficiency notice issued	March-April
Objections / Petition	May-June
Settlement Process	
Settlement discussions with the IRS	March
Tax team meeting to agree settlement parameters	March
Finalization of plan settlements	End March

Conclusion

IN ADDITION TO the above, the report will include the estimated budget to execute the TRM™ process. Usually an amount of approximately 1% of the quantified tax risk exposure is budgeted to fund the resources required to complete the initial implementation phase and leading up to the IRS sign-off of the on-the-radar screen issues and the successful shelving of the current off-the-radar screen issue.

Progress in the TRM™ process is monitored through ongoing tax steering committee meetings held as frequently as required, with the appropriate agenda.

The conclusion of the initial implementation process sees the ongoing management process being carried forward through the TRM™ Web interface into the future (refer to chapter 7 for full details of the system).

Set the Tax Risk Objectives for the Future

SETTING TAX RISK objectives in the development of a long-term plan in delivering the tax risk management TRM™ process should involve looking at two risk objectives—those at the strategic level and those that are operational. The strategic objectives will relate to the high-level goals set out in the TRM™ strategy; the operational objectives will be around what happens on a day-to-day basis. Examples include the following:

❑ The tax manager must take responsibility for tax risk management issues with tax team (strategic objective)

❑ Implement tax planning strategies that will impact positively on the day-to-day business (strategic objective)

❑ Improve relationships with the IRS (strategic objective)

❑ Finalize on- and off-the-radar screen issues (operational objective)

❑ Limit the number of tax planning ideas in any one period (operational objective)

❑ Ensure that the tax manager is involved in any new transactions, operations, or changes in financial accounting above a certain predetermined limit (operational objective)

❑ External opinions must be obtained on any tax risk issues over a predetermined value (operational objective)

❑ The total provisioned tax risk should not exceed a predetermined percentage of the annual tax charge (e.g., 10%) (operational objective)

❑ The cost of any IRS audit must not exceed a predetermined percentage of the tax payable (e.g., 3%) (operational objective)

❑ Penalties for any reason on tax issues should not exceed a predetermined percentage (e.g., 1%) (operational objective)

Communication: Again!

SETTING TAX RISK strategic and operational objectives will determine where resources are to be focused and directed. When these objectives have been established they should be documented and communicated to the tax team in the business and those who are involved in delivering them. These objectives should be built into their individual performance objectives. They effectively become the target in designing suitable tax risk management controls. It is also useful to develop a common means of documenting and communicating the tax risk objectives to create familiarity with the information throughout the business.

Chapter 4

Insular? Become More Transparent

Executive Summary

THE FOLLOWING TABLE is an extract from a survey conducted on www.7taxrisks.com over a period of two years and demonstrates the fact that the function of tax compliance within businesses is very insular and lacks the requisite interaction with other key persons in the business.

No documented tax strategy	78%
No regular monthly communication between tax compliance officer and heads of transactions	50%
No regular monthly communication between tax compliance officer and heads of operation	60%
Does the board discuss tax strategy and tax planning: mostly never or don't know	70%

The tax compliance officer is usually from an accounting background and compiles his or her information based on the financial information he or she receives from other people. The problem with this is that the tax compliance officer is not always in the position to communicate with the authors of this information so as to get to the "tax truth."

A system must be created which allows the easy flow of information to the tax compliance officer of more information based on the "raw facts."

Tax compliance must be broadened to include a wider TRM™ process, where the interaction with the IRS is more carefully planned. Tax mistakes should be identified and self-disclosed long before the IRS decides to audit. If there is any interaction with the IRS, ensure their full compliance with the laws and regulations that govern them, to ensure that they go about their business in a fair, reasonable, transparent, unbiased, and accountable manner. All these words are pregnant with meaning and must be carefully applied by taxpayers against the IRS in dealing with the technical merits of any IRS audit or investigation. Often members of the tax team will be able to give guidance on technical, procedural, strategic, and tactical aspects of any interaction with the IRS.

By remaining insular in the approach to tax risk and tax compliance, the businesses will only cause long-term financial distress which could have been avoided by employing some of the principles mentioned in this special report.

Introduction

CHAPTERS 1, 2, and 3 have brought the tax risk management process to a point where a TRM™ strategy is in existence, with a participating tax team and a positive attitude toward proactive tax risk management. This entire process for small businesses is taken care of through the tax-Radar™ program and the completion of the Tax Risk Matrix with the small businesses accounting firm.

This chapter deals with TRM™ Step 4.

Insular tax compliance from an ivory tower or by third parties handling your tax affairs can only mean that tax compliance is probably at its lowest, despite attempts to ensure the opposite by businesses. All key stakeholders must be involved from the CEO, the BO/CFO, the business owner, the board, and the audit committee to the outside legal team and tax advisors. In the case of small businesses this will be the business owner, the accountant, and the tax-Radar™ program. Tax managers are often left on their own and expected to remain on top of tax compliance, law, and regulatory changes and the management of a complex series of relationships throughout the organization so as to get to the "tax truth" in many transactions, financial accounting, and operation areas. Their ability to be totally transparent, so as to limit ongoing exposure to IRS, revised assessments, is stifled by their lack of authority to access all key areas of the business and outside advice, in areas that go beyond technical tax issues. Allowing transparency and connectivity into the mix turns the insular tax compliance problem around.

Tax Managers Do Not Know Everything

THE HEADING IS not stated lightly. It is also not meant to be an insult, but the fact is, tax managers need to get all the help they can muster in managing the tax risk of the business. This ranges from the business owner, the CEO through the BO/CFO to outside specialists, and in the case of small businesses, the tax-Radar™ program. This chapter gives direction on certain issues that are not known by many tax managers.

What the Big Boys Say

ONE OF THE larger accounting firms in the USA have given the following advice to businesses, as reported in Yahoo! Finance:

> "Corporations understand that new financial and tax requirements promise to change the way companies manage everything from Operations to IT," explains Mark Weinberg, Americas Vice Chair for Tax Services at Ernst & Young LLP. "We counsel Tax Directors to focus on **ten key steps** that will help them plan the way they manage tax risk and thereby affect the risk profile of the enterprise . . .
>
> • Become aware of **regulatory changes**. In addition to keeping up with changes, it is important to know what approach peers are taking—in your industry and in your region. Gather information about emerging practices to help form policy within your own company. Organize this knowledge so it can be deciphered easily and used to create future plans.

- List all **prominent stakeholders**. From audit committees to operational department heads, stakeholders in tax risk will have their own agendas and issues. Start with a list of those who will directly affect or be directly affected by tax risk management. Then review how you relate to each, planning for optimal communication and cooperation.

- Confirm your understanding of the **overall enterprise-wide risk management systems**. Talk to the Chief Risk Officer if there is one. Read risk documents. Reach out to Operations, IT, Finance and Treasury, regulatory/compliance and transactions departments, all of which have risk issues and profiles. Review strategic documents: tax strategy, risk strategy and overall business strategy. Consider how they align and make appropriate adjustments to the tax strategy if necessary.

- With every new calendar year, it makes sense to **review and adjust tax department objectives**. This year, Tax Directors are finding it particularly useful to make sure that department objectives reflect all changing demands—both external and within the organization.

- Initially, each Tax Director should look at **SOX 404 compliance requirements** and create a list of to dos for proper documentation and testing. In addition, best practices will go beyond the 404 work to incorporate other elements of risk, such as compliance and operations. While SOX directly addresses financial reporting, other areas may indeed be the sources of risk.

- Sit down the BO/CFO before the quarter closes to discuss **challenges, opportunities and objectives**. This may seem obvious, but it is critical if your new direction for the next tax year is to be in line with expectations. With proper direction, all tax activity in the next tax year will stay on focus.

- Become involved in **communicating with the audit committee**. Many audit committee meetings occur in

February and March, making January the time to get yourself on the agenda to present the mission of the Tax Department on your own terms.

- **Upgrade the definition of tax risk** to incorporate the enterprise definition of risk. This is also a time to make sure "risk" includes the potential to lose out on opportunities, such as making the tax function perform more efficiently.

- Start early to **review files of major transactions**, which will need to be in audit-ready condition. An initial review of the file will help prepare you for any extra work required in that area.

- Look at the **Tax Department operating model** and make sure activities are robust enough to meet the demands of the next tax year, such a compliance or financial reporting. If not, this will need to be addressed as you move into the first quarter."

A Dead Expense

> "To be conscious that you are ignorant is a great step to knowledge."
>
> Source: Benjamin Disraeli

INSULAR TAX RISK management starts with the lack of understanding of tax risks from the business owner, the CEO, to the BO/CFO, the tax manager, the in-house legal counsel, the outside tax advisors, transaction managers, operations managers, and financial managers. In fact, insular TRM™ is the product of no communication. The business owner or CEO doesn't want legal counsel involved with the tax manager, because it costs time and money. The tax manager doesn't want outside interference in an already-pressurized job.

The business owner or BO/CFO believes that all appropriate tax risks will surface when they are supposed to, because the outside tax advisers or accountants will eventually get there. Doing anything will only result in extra resources and spending more money—it is classified as a nonproductive dead expense!

This shortsighted outlook is immediately resolved for small businesses by participating in the tax-Radar™ program, in exchange for a small monthly commitment to cover the compilation of the Tax Risk Matrix, its ongoing maintenance, and full representation from the time of any IRS engagement until the matter is completed in the tax court or by settlement.

The 40/60 Rule

> *"Ignorance when it is voluntary is criminal."*
>
> Source: Samuel Johnson

THE SIMPLE ANSWER to these attitudes is to make a calculated "guesstimate" based on an article written by John A. Stacey (a leader at Deloitte in the area of tax risk management) in the article "Managing Tax Risk: Weighing Risk, Opportunity, and Transparency in a More Restrictive Regulatory and Government Environment" where he states,

Tax risk is certainly not limited to issues that arise with taxing authorities. Such a perspective not only limits the scope of potential tax risk, but may also result in an after-the-fact rather than a prospective management of that risk. It is also important to note that areas of potential tax risk are not restricted to transactions and processes under the direct authority of the corporate tax function. **An educated guess suggests that the tax function does not directly or exclusively manage more than 25 to 30 percent of tax risks in a given organization.** Clear areas of responsibility include tax accounting and compliance processes (such as the preparation of tax forms and tax provisions); tax-reduction planning initiated by the tax group and the monitoring of externally generated risks such as changes in tax and business laws and practices.

That being said, where is the remaining 75 percent of tax risk generated? As noted previously, it can be found in the business units and functional areas over which the tax function may have, at best, an oversight or dotted-line responsibility when tax issues arise.

The gap that exists between active tax oversight on approximately 25 percent of risks and the remaining 75 percent is the crux of the challenge. The Sarbanes-Oxley and other equivalent rules apply to the design and effective operation of the company's internal controls and procedures over "financial reporting"—thereby encompassing every process that touches the reported results. A vast array of taxes, both direct and indirect, is a very important determinant of shareholder value and earnings per share.

In making a conservative adjustment to the Stacey guesstimate, if one assumes that about 40% of a business's tax risk is covered by the usual tax compliance functions, 60% or more is not. What does this translate to?

Assuming your business tax bill for the last year was $4m or $40m or $400m, and this is only 40% of the actual tax liability covered, your business could be facing an additional $6m, $60m, or $600m uncovered tax bill based on the 40/60 rule.

How is it possible to reach $6m, $60m, or $600m? If the Revenue discovers a tax indiscretion of $100,000 for a year and is able to extrapolate the tax indiscretion over ten years, the revised assessment may start with revised tax of $1m capital. Add to this up to 75% penalties, the sum increases to just under $2m. Add to this interest over ten years, compounded, the sum could easily double up as just under $4m. One hundred thousand dollars per year, $1m per year, or $10m per year, depending on the size of the business. The taxes that could have problems are direct (income) taxes and indirect (VAT, sales tax, and payroll) tax. A real possibility exists that a sum to the estimated 60% uncovered tax may exist. Either way, you cannot afford not to make sure and reverse an insular attitude to tax. Focusing on the problem will help!

Transparency

> *"An old-fashioned handshake is a good way to do business—unless the*
> IRS *demands a copy"*
>
> Source: Cullen Hightower

> *"The condition of being obvious or evident."*
>
> Source: Oxford Dictionary

IN THIS DAY and age it is important that businesses take a more open-minded approach when it comes to tax compliance.

The process of transparency is not confined to the completion of a tax return and the disclosure made to the IRS. It begins with transparency between the role players involved in a transaction, the key decision makers in the business, and the people responsible for understanding the tax implications and compiling the return. Taxpayers who are aware of the disclosing requirements of transactions are in a better position to avoid unnecessary taxes, additional taxes, interest, and penalties later on.

Transparent tax compliance is an essential element in obtaining finality of assessments issued by the IRS. Most tax legislation will empower the IRS to raise an additional assessment against a taxpayer at any time, even though an original assessment has already been raised, and the time period has lapsed where that original assessment has become final and conclusive. This leads to uncertainty in respect of a taxpayer's tax exposure. Fortunately, this tax legislation does not usually give the IRS carte blanche in that it will usually limit the authority of the IRS to reopen an assessment and raise an additional assessment only after the IRS has satisfied itself of the fact that an amount that should have been assessed to tax was not so assessed due to fraud, misrepresentation, or nondisclosure of material facts. Unlike fraud and misrepresentation, nondisclosure of material facts could be an innocent mistake which nevertheless results in adverse tax consequences well after the original tax assessment has become final and conclusive.

Inadequate Tax Disclosure Comes from Lack of Knowledge

MORE OFTEN THAN not, inadequate disclosure is the result of a lack of knowledge into a transaction on the part of the person compiling the tax return and not necessarily as a result of reluctance to fully disclose the transaction. This "lack of knowledge" could be overcome by having access to all the facts pertaining to a material transaction. It will ultimately lead to the person preparing the tax return being in a better position to complete the return, ensuring adequate disclosure and handling any queries. Accessibility to facts could be achieved by hands-on record keeping in the form of files containing all the documents in respect of a material transaction, i.e., agreements, memoranda, minutes of meetings, resolutions, opinions, and correspondence. A complete understanding of the facts will include interaction between the various role players in a transaction, the key decision makers, and the tax department.

Inadequate disclosure can also be as a result of a lack of understanding of the detail required when a particular transaction is disclosed. The question arises as to what constitutes adequate disclosure? How much information needs to be provided to the IRS before a transaction has been adequately disclosed? One would think that a taxpayer can accept that the duty rests on the IRS and its officials to ask the necessary questions and call for the necessary supporting documentation in order for them to unravel the finer details of a taxpayer's affairs. This, however, is often not the case as the courts are reluctant to expect the IRS such a degree of diligence.

In one South African tax case (ITC 1459) the meaning of "material facts" was interpreted by the court as follows: the court laid down a simple test to determine whether certain facts were material. It considered the information furnished subsequent to the tax authority's inquiries regarding the present transaction and compared that information with the detail in the returns including their supporting documents. It was held that from the lack of detail provided in the return it was obvious that the IRS or its officer did not have all the material facts. It was the absence of those facts which led to the issue of the original assessments. In addition the court held that it is no answer to say that the tax authority should have been alerted by what it saw, or was able to see, in the return and accompanying documents. The question is whether the tax authority had all the material facts when it issued the original assessment. It does not matter that the tax authority's ignorance was partly due to a failure to make inquiries before issuing the original assessment.

In another South African tax case (ITC 1594) it was held that an obligation rests upon a taxpayer to render an accurate and full return on which he can be assessed and not to do so in a vague or ambiguous manner casting the onus upon the tax authority to elicit the complete picture by a series of queries.

Ticked Boxes?

IT IS THEREFORE clear that it cannot simply be accepted that ticking the correct boxes and submitting the required supporting schedules is sufficient. A taxpayer is required to provide the IRS with all the material facts which would influence their decision on how the transaction should be treated for tax purposes. The crucial time to provide this information is before the original assessment is issued. The best opportunity is therefore in the tax return.

Cooperation between Senior Management and the Tax Manager

TRANSPARENT TAX COMPLIANCE means that the IRS will find it very difficult to issue an additional assessment after the expiry of the statutory final and conclusive period to close an original assessment. This is a strategy worth considering but can only be accomplished when all the key decision makers within an organization (for instance, the CEO, the BO/CFO, and the tax manager), the role players in a particular transaction, and the audit committee take an active interest in and work together with the tax department in achieving this.

Case of Checking Information

FOR INSTANCE, A tax compliance officer in a large corporation recently decided to review over a period of sixty minutes the tax pack reports submitted to him by the financial manager that had excluded certain deductions which had been deducted for accounting purposes. There were numerous such situations giving rise to "disallowable deductions" of over $2 million. On closer examination by the tax compliance officer he discovered that all the financial managers had made the same mistake. Expenses they wanted to disallow for tax purposes were all for marketing purposes and were clearly deductible, but they had been marked not deductible, because certain employees who enjoyed these benefits had not been subjected to fringe benefit tax. The two concepts are completely different, and there was no reason to not deduct the expenses albeit the need to look at the fringe benefits.

What Does It Mean When a Taxpayer Receives an IRS Query?

GENERALLY, WHEN A taxpayer receives an IRS query, IRS intends auditing the taxpayer's tax affairs.

Such a query generally takes the form of a written notification to the taxpayer in terms of which the taxpayer is requested to provide IRS with certain information and documentation relating to either a specific transaction or to specific tax years.

The query may include an investigation of all the relevant taxes applicable to the taxpayer, such as income tax, value-added tax, sales tax, PAYE, and payroll taxes.

Is the IRS Entitled to Request Information and Documentation from Taxpayers?

THE EMPOWERING LEGISLATION that gives the IRS the power to administer and collect taxes will provide that IRS with the authority to require a taxpayer or any person to furnish information, whether orally or in writing, documents or things, to that IRS.

It must be understood that this is a compelling provision which taxpayers are in general required to adhere to. But make sure that the IRS has applied the provisions of the empowering legislation correctly, failing which the taxpayer would have a good reason not to comply. Legal guidance should be sought on this before such a bold step is taken by the taxpayer.

Where information or documentation is not provided by a taxpayer, the IRS can issue a criminal summons. It should be noted that failure to comply may constitute a criminal offence unless good cause is shown why the taxpayer is not complying. But seek legal advice before being difficult with the IRS.

What Should Taxpayers Do When the IRS Queries Their Tax Affairs?

FIRSTLY, IT IS recommended that any request for information or documentation be reduced to writing as this will help set the parameters of the audit going forward.

The taxpayer should also check which tax years are involved and which taxes.

Where the IRS requests information beyond a typical three-year period, a defense may lie under the appropriate tax provision that a statutory limitation period may apply where a taxpayer may successfully argue that it does not have to provide any information or documentation, as the period for raising any additional assessments may have prescribed in that the original tax assessment has become final and conclusive. Obviously, the taxpayer must be confident that it had been properly transparent when the original tax return was submitted to the IRS.

For the IRS to go beyond a three-year period, they would usually have to show that there has been fraud, misrepresentation, or nondisclosure on the part of the taxpayer.

The IRS can also be requested to advise for what specific purpose, in terms of the appropriate tax legislation, the inquiry is being conducted.

These requirements are usually spelt out in the relevant tax legislation. Any conduct by the IRS that falls outside the scope of their powers, as specifically legislated, may entitle the taxpayer to review their conduct in court.

How Would a Taxpayer Know If They Are Also the Subject of a Criminal Investigation?

GENERALLY, THE IRS will not advise taxpayers that they are also the subject of a criminal investigation when they commence with a civil audit of the taxpayer's tax affairs.

Herein lies the problem in that a taxpayer may provide the IRS with information or documentation pursuant to the compelling provisions of tax legislation that the IRS may subsequently attempt to use against the taxpayer in a criminal investigation once the civil audit has been finalized.

A remedy may lie in favor of such a taxpayer which can successfully argue that the information or documentation they provided was under compulsion. The taxpayer could then state that as the information was given under compulsion, it had not waived its right not to self-incriminate itself. Any evidence obtained by a criminal investigation department under such circumstances would arguably be inadmissible evidence given that the taxpayer has a right not to incriminate itself and to remain silent in accordance with most constitutions.

Any information or documentation given to the IRS should clearly be marked that the information is given to the IRS under the compelling provisions of the relevant tax legislation and as such does not constitute admissible evidence against the taxpayer, other than for the IRS to make a revised assessment of tax in terms of a civil audit.

In any event, when an audit is engaged by the IRS, an attempt should be made to determine the precise nature of the investigation into the taxpayer's affairs.

What Can Be Expected at the End of an IRS Query?

THE PURPOSE OF an audit by the IRS is to verify the taxpayer's tax affairs with their hope of ultimately raising an additional assessment.

Once the exchange of information and documentation has been completed, the IRS must be requested to provide a letter of findings prior to any additional assessment being raised, in which they should explain in clear and certain terms the facts that they are relying upon in coming to their decision and precisely which sections of the tax legislation they propose to apply.

It should be made clear that a taxpayer is entitled to such a letter of findings and that the taxpayer should have an opportunity to respond thereto prior to any additional assessments being raised.

It is a good idea to meet with the IRS so that they can discuss the letter of findings with the taxpayer. It is also a good idea to take the IRS through the taxpayer's response to the letter of findings so that the parties can attempt to ultimately agree on the additional assessments to be raised, if any.

The Case of Furs and Pelts Ltd.

THE IRS had completed its on-site audit at the headquarters of Furs and Pelts Ltd. at the end of April. At the end of May the taxpayer received an eleven-page letter of findings, listing seven areas that the IRS believed the company had erred in its tax compliance. The IRS was intending to issue a revised assessment of close to $80m within a matter of days. This excluded penalties and interest.

Professional Consultants were, at the very last minute, asked to assist in responding to the letter of findings. The following urgent course of action was followed:

With the deadline looming, a courtesy call was made to the IRS to arrange an urgent face-to-face meeting to discuss their findings.

The meeting took place early in June. The attendees for the company were the tax advisory team, the financial manager of the company, a tax lawyer, and a tax forensic accountant. The IRS audit team and their legal representatives were also present.

At the meeting, Professional Consultants explained that they had just been briefed on the matter and had not even had a proper opportunity to consider all the facts and applicable law, as well as the substance of the letter of findings. Accordingly, in order to allow the taxpayer to exercise its rights by responding comprehensively to the IRS's findings, Professional Consultants requested an extension in which to conduct its own thorough investigation and compare their findings with that of the IRS.

Although the tone of the meeting was amicable, the IRS was disinclined to grant any further indulgences. Professional Consultants emphasized that the request for time was not a dilatory tactic but merely a concerted effort to perform an internal audit. It was emphasized that the taxpayer was in no way trying to evade tax—where the taxpayer was at fault and liable for any outstanding taxes, it would pay the IRS. Where, however, Professional Consultants' findings differed from those of the IRS, a presentation with all the necessary explanations and accurate calculations would be made in an effort to disprove the IRS's findings.

The IRS eventually agreed to grant an extension on condition that once the period had elapsed, Professional Consultants was to present its findings so that the matter could be finalized. Throughout the meeting it was clear that the IRS had a significant amount to collect on their potential assessment and thus was eager to get it issued so that collection proceedings could begin. Because so much was riding on the assessment,

Professional Consultants had to caution the IRS that even once the presentation had been furnished, it was the IRS's responsibility to allow the taxpayer a fair and reasonable opportunity to discharge its onus and, in so doing, disprove the IRS's findings. It was reiterated that the IRS had a duty to interact with the taxpayer and not hastily issue the assessment without due consideration of any discrepancies. Therefore, it was not sufficient for the IRS to simply disagree with the taxpayer, they had to provide adequate reasons why their findings were correct and the taxpayer's were inaccurate.

It was essential that the parameters of the relationship between the parties were clearly and meticulously discussed and recorded. The entire meeting was taped and then transcribed, and the typed minutes were circulated to the IRS for approval. This was crucial because at a later stage when the IRS denied having agreed to certain things and threatened to raise the assessment, the minutes were referred to; and nobody could dispute the accuracy contained therein since everyone had, or were expected to have, read and agreed to the contents.

Immediately thereafter, Professional Consultants compiled a plan of action to be executed within the strict time constraint they had. This involved examining each and every issue the IRS had identified and allocating the correct person from the legal team to that specific investigation.

Accountants and auditors were selected to perform detailed audits in respect of all the taxes under scrutiny. Because the audit was so substantial and would be extremely time consuming and demanding on resources, team leaders were chosen who, in turn, had a number of clerks under their supervision to assist in the data capturing.

The legal team was instructed to start collating the entire history of the matter and carry out interviews with all the key role players. This meant interviewing all the taxpayer's staff members who had liaised with IRS and/or furnished information during their initial audit and then recording a detailed chronology of events.

Once the accounting leg was complete, the calculations were explained to the legal team who then had to marry the accounting principles with the legal principles in an effort to give plausible and understandable explanations to the results.

It was a mammoth task, but with the right resources in place, it was implemented professionally and expeditiously. Eventually, after working around the clock to finish the investigation timeously, it became apparent that all of the IRS's findings were incorrect and based on the wrong principles. The next hurdle was to reduce everything to writing in a presentation which would clearly illustrate the taxpayer's calculations and, in so doing, convince the IRS that the taxpayer was right and should not be assessed.

The presentation was pedantically drafted. The introduction comprised a detailed history of the events leading up to the IRS's letter of findings. Thereafter, each issue was addressed by demonstrating first what the IRS's findings were, and what they were based on, and then doing the same for the taxpayer, ending off with why the IRS had erred in their findings. Professional Consultants made sure that all supplementary evidence was included in the presentation so that the IRS had all the relevant information and documentation before them to be persuaded.

All the parties then convened in a meeting in order for Professional Consultants to make a verbal presentation to the IRS, together with a submission of the hard copy. During this presentation, each professional who was responsible for their specific investigation took the IRS through their audit and corresponding calculations and answered any questions posed. The aim was to prove that the basis of the taxpayer's audit was accurately performed so that no uncertainty could be placed on the outcome.

The presentation also contained technical arguments revolving around procedure and the burden of proof. Here Professional Consultants indicated that the standard of inquiry was on a balance of probabilities which the taxpayer had satisfied. Consequently, it had discharged its onus and the IRS had to consider retracting its letter of findings.

Obviously the IRS did not appreciate the fact that all their hard work had been refuted and that the huge assessment they were anticipating would need to be reconsidered. Because of this underlying dissatisfaction, it became very difficult to persuade the IRS representatives who had performed the initial audit. They simply rejected Professional Consultants' arguments but failed to substantiate why. Once again, Professional Consultants pointed out that adequate reasons had to be furnished by the IRS, and it was not sufficient to merely disagree. In the absence of such reasons, it was pointed out that the only conclusion to be drawn by the taxpayer (and a court of law if necessary) was that the findings were arrived at without due consideration of the facts and law and without proper application of mind. Under the circumstances, no objective person or judge would allow an assessment to stand, and the procedure applied in trying to get the assessment issued would be materially flawed, and the conduct of the IRS could be taken on review.

It was imperative to politely convey this to the IRS so they were aware of the implications their action could have and the rights the taxpayer could pursue if the matter remained unresolved. Eventually, the IRS responded that they would need to perform another audit on all the taxpayer's files, comparing their investigation at all stages with Professional Consultants.

The taxpayer was more than willing to assist in this regard and transported all the boxes of all their documents to Professional Consultants offices where the IRS were invited to carry out their audit. It was important to have the files at the advisors' premises so that they could oversee the IRS's progress and answer any questions as and when they arose. The instruction was for the IRS auditors to query things immediately and not jump to conclusions based on unfounded inferences. Professional Consultants explained that this was the mistake in the first instance, namely, the IRS did not work together with the taxpayer's representatives during their initial investigation and so came to erroneous conclusions. Had they discussed the issues there and then, a lot of queries could have been resolved and much of the issues raised in the letter of findings could have been avoided. Because Professional Consultants had indicated this was the problem with the audit, the IRS had warned their auditors to be thorough and proceed on an interactive basis (one can imagine they needed to save face and try to salvage as much of their findings as possible).

After several weeks, IRS informed the taxpayer that they needed to take the files to their premises as they would require more time and resources. Professional Consultants agreed as the files were housed in a completely separate room with dedicated auditors.

Professional Consultants kept following up and requesting feedback, but the IRS merely replied that they were still working on the matter and would revert in due course.

To date, the taxpayer and its advisors are still waiting for the IRS to revert, and no assessment has ever been issued. This result was almost unbelievable in hindsight, but the taxpayer did the right thing—it instructed legal advisors to handle the matter instead of trying to deal with it internally. What the taxpayer thought initially they could handle by themselves turned into a disaster and could have been prevented if the legal team were introduced from the outset. Notwithstanding this, the team was brought in just in time to get the matter back on track, and the positive result was certainly appreciated by the taxpayer's representatives who fully believed that their business would close down because of the exorbitant assessment. This taxpayer has certainly learnt from their mistake and now knows to call in their legal team as soon as they receive any query from the IRS. This will ensure that communications are dealt with properly from the beginning and that the correct procedure is implemented and maintained to ensure all matters are accurately resolved. In addition, a legal team will know what arguments to submit on the taxpayer's behalf to facilitate a successful outcome. Without an advisory team's expert guidance, taxpayers could find themselves in situations which could have been prevented had the right measures been in place.

Legitimate Expectations

AS TO THE meaning of a legitimate expectation, take a look at the "TRM™ Dictionary" at the beginning of this special report. Its practical significance comes from the advice a taxpayer will get from a legal team that is alive to new possibilities and defenses. When preparing for any defense on a tax inquiry from the IRS, the key starting point is the facts—all the facts. Then marry the facts to the legislative provisions and any enlightening case law. Now there is an additional opportunity. How has the IRS publicly interpreted the tax provisions? Have they published any practice notes for clarification? If so, these public statements can be relied upon by the taxpayer in any defense, being a legitimate expectation in favor of the taxpayer, that cannot just be ignored by the IRS, from a procedural point of view. They are bound to their statements and can only change them into the future.

Chapter 5
More Facts Resolve Tax Risks

Executive Summary

TAXPAYERS NEED TO be in possession of the facts surrounding any transaction that a business is entering into. If the facts are not readily available, go and find them!

It is no misconception that the nature of transactions varies considerably from the time of inception until they are signed off and finalized. The opinion that is often obtained at the inception stage should always be used as a guiding factor. However, due to the intricacies of many transactions, the opinion obtained may only be relevant in part with respect to the end result. Taking this into consideration it is imperative to conduct a post legal and tax audit. This is primarily for the organization to take it upon itself to determine whether the opinions set out in the initial documentation still stand in the final drafts. Experts should be brought in at the beginning, middle, and end of such transactions.

All your bases must be covered in order to explain, should you have to, the nature of the transaction in the years to come. It is no mystery that some transactions may be investigated five to ten years down the line. Record keeping can often make or break a taxpayer's case when it comes to such investigations. This is why posttransaction audits must be carried out in order for you to track down and maintain records, thereby allowing you to be fully prepared should the IRS come knocking on a taxpayer's door down the line.

Introduction

IN CHAPTERS 1 to 4, executing a proactive tax risk management plan, with the tax team following a TRM™ strategy, and the tax manager ensuring that he or she is accessing maximum external input, outside his or her ivory tower, the necessity for more facts becomes increasingly evident. This chapter deals with TRM™ Step 5 and those "more facts!"

Lack of facts, facts, and more facts often leads to bad tax compliance and unnecessary mistakes that could have been avoided. Getting to the bottom of the facts takes time and effort and is the most important starting point in any TRM™ strategy implementation. Thereafter the technical expertise can be applied properly. Large transactions illustrate this point time and time again as businesses continuously fail to check the facts, check the advice, then check the facts again.

In the case of small businesses that are participating in the tax-Radar™ program, this is one area that the business owner cannot delegate. The business owner must spend some time in revisiting all the potential tax risk areas in the business to ensure that proper facts and information are given to the accountant to place on the Tax Risk Matrix. If this is not done properly tax risks that are present will not be identified and will cause potential greater harm to that business. The proper completion of the Tax Risk Matrix at inception is of paramount importance.

Facts, Facts, and More Facts!

THIS IS THE single most important factor in eliminating tax risk into the future and eliminating the tax risks of the past. Get to the bottom of all the facts.

If they don't exist anymore, go and find them from a person who can give you a clear statement about what happened in the past—but get the facts.

With a clear set of facts, the law can be meticulously checked and applied to the best advantage of the taxpayer. Tax risks can be accurately determined, and a strategy can be devised to minimize the exposure.

Without the facts, the taxpayer is at the mercy of an IRS that may jump to conclusions in the absence of the facts.

Where Does Transactional Tax Risk Come From?

TRANSACTIONAL TAX RISK entails assessing the tax risks associated with the various steps taken in major transactions by businesses. Some of the most obvious tax risks are the tax antiavoidance provisions in tax legislation, "connected persons," controlled foreign entity legislation, transfer pricing, and simulated transactions. But there are many more. The more unusual the transaction, the greater the tax risk. Typical transactions that require the facts to be carefully collected and subjected to a legal and tax audit include acquisitions, mergers, demergers, management buyouts, and structured finance deals. Often much effort goes into planning a transaction, but then there is lack of attention to detail in the implementation of the transaction, and double-checking the implementation after the transaction is concluded. Usually the transaction is dealt with properly from an accounting perspective. But then little is done by way of a closing legal audit and compiling a collection of relevant documents, archived properly, with opinions at the ready to respond to any queries by the IRS. The legal audit ensures compliance with the original planned structure, supported by the various opinions.

Typically tax risks can result from transactions in some of the following instances:

❑ The IRS successfully challenges the technical basis of the tax treatment of the transaction. Such a challenge can be averted by holding unqualified and positive opinions from leading tax specialists, where the taxpayer has also made certain that the implementation of the transaction ties up with the opinion or advice given.

❑ The analysis of a step in the transaction is dependent on an accounting treatment that is not accepted by the IRS. This challenge can also be averted with opinions.

❑ A change in the tax laws affects the transaction before it matures. To overcome this tax risk, the transaction must be revisited every year.

❏ The tax treatment adopted and arguments used to support one transaction are inconsistent or prejudice arguments in another counter or similar transaction. Once again, the overall effect of the steps in a transaction, and its tax effect in counter or similar transactions, must be considered at the time of planning. If this is not done properly, multiple transactions may fail as a result of a single technical failure, giving rise to significant tax risk in the transaction.

❏ If the transaction is not implemented as planned, it will result in the failure to meet a question of fact. If that key fact does not exist, as an assumption in the opinion supporting the transaction, the transaction may fail, resulting in the tax consequences originally feared.

❏ There is operational or administrative failure through key aspects of the transaction not being properly recorded for tax on an ongoing basis, resulting in misrepresentation or nondisclosure to the IRS, which may cause additional tax risk.

❏ The transaction prejudices the relationship with the IRS, and publicity adversely affects the reputation of the business with the IRS. Many analysts place a high premium on the tax reputation of a business when assessing it for business.

❏ Can explanations be given for the tax planning being implemented with a transaction? Will this attract the attention of the IRS when compared to the IRS's perceived high tax risk areas?

❏ Is the taxpayer confident that the advice that has been given on the tax issues is objective and soundly based?

❏ Are there any tax skeletons in newly acquired entities? Has an appropriate tax due diligence been done?

❏ Are the tax outcomes in line with the business outcomes?

❏ Have transactions been properly valued and adequately recorded?

❏ If the transaction implemented is complicated, is this because the business issues are complex as well?

❑ Are additional steps designed to reduce taxes that would ordinarily be payable?

The starting point in answering all these questions, and getting to grips with the level of tax risk, is to carefully analyze all facts surrounding the transaction.

Why Do Transactions Go Wrong?

BY WAY OF introduction, these are some of the principles that taxpayers must be made aware of and know in order to approach any complex investigation by the Revenue into any transactions.

Any audit by the IRS must be prefaced by a fundamental question asked by the BO/CFO and the CEO in the taxpayer entity: "What is the business's internal tax strategy?" From various surveys that have been conducted online at www.7taxrisks.com it is clear that the majority of the survey participants do not have a tax strategy. The majority of the participants also do not discuss tax strategy or even broader tax issues at board level. Many of these businesses are not entirely sure whether or not they are 100% tax compliant and in line with these concerns. Many of these businesses have not undergone recent IRS audits.

In larger businesses, responsible for making large tax payments, it is a matter of time before the IRS ends up knocking on their door. In addition to this, if that business is unable to answer positively that they have a tax strategy, or that they are 100% certain that they are fully tax compliant, the business will end up facing large revised assessments relative to the profit of the business.

A Payroll Audit Tax Exposure

TAKE AS AN example a payroll audit; the starting point would be let's say a transgression of $50,000 per year. If the IRS takes this transgression and extrapolate the noncompliance amount back over the last ten years, the tax bill jumps to $500,000. Add to this 75% penalties and the tax bill increases to nearly $1m. Add to this interest over a ten-year period and the outstanding tax could double to $2m. The business now immediately becomes a debtor and owes this money to the State, placing the taxpayer entity into a very embarrassing position. This position is compounded, and the company ends up having to defend its position because the moment the revised assessment is issued the IRS will take action. They will typically hand the matter over to their collections department and immediately start demanding that the amount be paid. Now the company is constantly on the back foot trying to postpone or trying to make arrangements to pay the amount of revised tax, despite the fact that the company may feel very strongly that it owes nothing or very little.

At this stage, if the PNAL principle (pay now argue later principle applied in Canada, South Africa, and many other jurisdictions) is not suspended through the intervention of the legal team, the company may end up facing severely hard financial times.

With Hindsight Mistakes Are Easily Fixed with Facts

WHAT COULD HAPPEN is that the mistake picked up by the IRS is one that can so easily have been fixed had the mistake been identified soon enough. In payroll tax risk areas the mistake is often made that the employment agreement fails to reflect, in writing, new salary arrangements implemented by the salary administration department. All that remains to be done is the systematic resigning of addendums to the original employment agreements to give effect to the clear intentions between employer and employee.

Many companies at this point, by virtue of pressure from their boards of directors, who up until now have known virtually nothing about the dispute, have never discussed any tax strategy or dispute or risk issues at their board meetings or even in some of their audit committee meetings, will typically now try and push the tax department to reach some kind of settlement so as to get rid of this new tax liability. These pressures to push for settlement will come from nonexecutive board members who would have been involved in similar disputes in other companies and will come back with the information saying that the IRS may be prepared to settle, hence the pressure to get around a settlement table and settle. The reality is that the taxpayers, due to this pressure, will end up settling for an amount less than the $3m, but often for an amount far more than what would have been the case if they had remedied the source of the problem through a carefully planned TRM™ process.

The example based on a payroll tax audit is of course no different from investigations that takes place into other transactions by the IRS.

Question Processes Internally and the IRS

TO AVOID SOME of the real tax risks that may flow from an audit conducted by the IRS into various transactions, the following questions need to be asked:

❑ What tax strategy is in place to fully investigate, understand, and analyze the major transactions which the business has entered into over the past ten years?

❑ Has this been discussed at audit committee or board level in any detail so that the audit committee members and the board members are clearly aware of the potential risks that face the business?

❑ Ask the IRS how many transactions of a similar nature are currently the subject of an investigation by them.

Of course, the problem with major historical transactions is that the potential tax liability will often not be as small as $3m. Bring that to the attention of the audit committee, and to the board, and again a huge amount of pressure will be applied to find a way of getting around to a settlement and negotiation table with the IRS to try and settle the revised tax amount, as opposed to trying to live with the liability on a balance sheet, and go forward into the formal dispute stages.

The question must then be asked, "How strong are the business's negotiation abilities to do this successfully?" Will the business have prepared itself to be in the best possible situation to negotiate the absolutely best settlement for itself? What complicates matters even more is that many large transactions have been driven by a variety of financial institutions which have their own agendas. They will also approach any IRS investigation in such a manner to protect their own interests first.

Taxpayers' Rights

IN LINE WITH the fundamental rights which often exist in favor of taxpayers through information and administration legislation in various jurisdictions, taxpayers can expect the IRS to be totally transparent in what they are doing in conducting an investigation into a historical transaction, insofar as it may affect another taxpayer. Usually a taxpayer cannot approach the IRS and ask them to provide information about another taxpayer. But a taxpayer can expect the IRS to be totally transparent on any investigation into its own affairs. Taxpayers would be well within their rights to ask the IRS, at the time that they commence any audit of any transaction, what information they already have at their disposal on the transaction in question. Often the IRS would have approached the auditors, the financial institution involved, and any other promoters involved in that transaction. The IRS can be asked to share what information has been provided by these entities as they affect the taxpayers, what questions have been answered, what questions have been put, and what information is still outstanding in respect of any questions or queries submitted to these third parties.

In this regard the TQQ in the "TRM™ Dictionary" at the beginning of this special report may be useful (please take note of the disclaimer at the end of the definition of TQQ at the beginning of this special report). The failure by the IRS to answer and address these questions may give rise to an opportunity to force them to do so under the appropriate information legislation. Such formal appeal will also give rise to a formidable defense against any threats by the IRS to ignore your questions and enforce their entitlement to information from you immediately. However, because a fundamental right exists in that the IRS must be transparent, a very good defense exists why the taxpayer does not have to provide any additional information until such time as the IRS has answered the reasonable and practical questions put to them.

Right up front and at the time that the IRS starts upon their audit, the business is able to turn the inquiry back to them, and the taxpayer is able to clarify at precisely what stage the inquiry is at. If their response is that they have not involved any third parties yet, the taxpayer can ask the question whether it is the intention of the IRS to actually approach these third parties to further the inquiry. It would be very difficult for the IRS to defend that it was not their intention to do so. Their response would probably be that once they have obtained the information they will then determine to what extent they will question other third parties. A possible reaction to this response would be to state that the taxpayer would like to provide as complete an answer as possible and that it is the intention of the taxpayer to make contact with appropriate third parties in addressing the questions asked by the IRS thoroughly. The IRS would find it difficult to refuse this, because the taxpayer would be able to demonstrate that the reason why this course of action is being pursued is to ensure that there is no duplication of time, expense, effort, and resources in answering the questions of the IRS.

Another fundamental right of taxpayers is to expect the IRS to give proper and adequate reasons why they are inquiring into the transaction. It is for this reason that questioning the IRS is important. The IRS can only raise an additional assessment if they are able to show on the facts at their disposal, as supported by the law, that an amount of tax is due.

However, while the inquiry is being questioned and answered, it will be difficult for the IRS to raise additional assessments, until they have proper and adequate reasons. The practical significance of following this process is that the audit process by the IRS will be slowed down significantly. This holds two advantages for the taxpayer. One is a tactical and strategic advantage, the other is one that goes to the very merits of the case. Let's deal with the latter one first.

By forcing the IRS to play open cards with the business and to be transparent as to what the investigation is all about, and with whom they have already communicated, the business is placed into a position where it can now specifically focus on the potential areas of concern and in this way narrow down the focus of the audit with the view to bringing it to a proper conclusion where proper time and effort is spent on those aspects that deserve attention without merely looking at a transaction which is being attacked from every conceivable direction. There is common sense in making sure that the IRS understands precisely where the IRS is coming from and precisely what their difficulty is with the transaction being investigated. To make any valid allegation the IRS must be sure of their facts and should have investigated all the documentation, including agreements between the parties to the transaction, in order to arrive at any conclusions suggesting a tax liability.

The tactical and strategic advantage is that by slowing down the audit process in respect of the transaction investigated, the taxpayer will place the IRS assessor team that is dealing with the matter under pressure. It is not uncommon for the IRS teams to have to complete an investigation within a set number of hours with the duty to produce a result in revised assessments. By engaging the assessor team in this exchange of very necessary correspondence, it is going to be highly unlikely that they will meet their budgeted hours deadline for this investigation. The immediate reaction by most people would then be to place this particular investigation at the bottom of the pile. This is not what the taxpayer necessarily wants to happen, because finality in an investigation like this is first prize.

The effect of this within the IRS must also be considered. Assessor teams change from time to time. People move around, people are promoted, people leave the IRS. It is therefore highly likely that in the fullness of time, the taxpayer may end up with one assessor team; and ultimately by the time the audit process is completed, they will be dealing with another assessor team. This holds advantages and disadvantages. The advantage is that the initial assessor team will lose some of its momentum in bringing their matter to finality. Every time a new assessor team is appointed, there will be a flurry of activity where they will attempt to try and bring the matter to finality only to be met with the same problems faced by the first assessor team. So the matter will probably be put to the bottom of the pile again. The ultimate result is that at some point in the future, someone in a senior position within the IRS will be prepared to approach the taxpayer and seek to settle the matter, unless it is clear that the IRS have no real case, in which event the audit will simply stop.

Immediately this happens, from a negotiation point of view, the taxpayer is in a much stronger position. Of course, one is dealing with people whose personalities can be unpredictable. Throughout this process it must be remembered why the taxpayer is questioning the IRS. To get to the bottom of the problem and to stop the IRS issuing quick revised assessments that immediately rushes the taxpayer onto a back foot. The taxpayer is disengaging the IRS from improper conduct on their part. It is important that the taxpayer is not in turn guilty of a similar transgression.

The bottom line is that taxpayers are entitled to question everything and are entitled to the maximum amount of information from the IRS. Use that right effectively with the view to ensuring that the taxpayer knows and understands what the IRS investigation is all about. This may mean that the usual process followed by most other major taxpayers or financial institutions is deviated from. Most advisors will maintain that this course of action is a waste of time and will merely irritate the IRS. Despite these negative sentiments, it should be remembered that taxpayers are entitled to exercise their rights. The IRS tend at times to ignore these rights and merely proceed with assessments. For the most part, many taxpayers are not aware of these rights.

The process explained above is a very effective one, and once the detail has been worked through by the IRS to the third parties involved in these transactions, the taxpayer will get to the truth from a perspective that will entitle the taxpayer to formulate the best settlement of the matter.

In the process of careful examination of the transaction, taxpayers may find that there are instances were the implementation of the transaction has not taken place properly in accordance with the original advice taken by advisors and the financial institution involved. If the transaction is not thoroughly investigated, these problems will not be exposed by the taxpayer, and therefore these problems will not be able to be remedied at this late stage.

The process explained is in response to an audit from the IRS. In a sense then it is already too late. Had the taxpayer embarked on a proper TRM™ process all the potentially contentious transactions would have been properly checked before and after their final execution. At that stage any mistakes could be exposed and fixed.

Legitimate Expectations Again!

> *"In English law, the concept of legitimate expectation arises from administrative law, a branch of public law. In proceedings for judicial review, it applies the principles of fairness and reasonableness to the situation where a person has an expectation or interest in a public body retaining a long-standing practice or keeping a promise."*
>
> Source: Wikipedia

AS ALREADY DEFINED in the "TRM™ Dictionary" at the beginning of this special report, legitimate expectations are a close relative of taxpayers' rights. So often IRS will publish notes of their practices or interpretation of a given tax provision in an attempt to create further clarity on what is already a difficult set of rules for taxpayers to abide by.

Although these practices and interpretations do not override promulgated tax laws, they do create something similar to a right in favor of the taxpayer against the IRS, if the taxpayer decides to follow the practice or interpretation placed by the IRS on the tax provision.

For instance, if the IRS were to publish the wear and tear rates applicable to specified assets, and these rates were accepted by the taxpayer, they would be binding on the IRS, despite the fact that their commissioner may have a discretion that can be applied to the period of a wear and tear allowance applicable to that taxpayer and the asset concerned.

Similarly, where the minister of finance has declared in a budget speech that taxpayers are encouraged to come forward voluntarily to own up on any tax transgressions without fear of criminal or penalty reprisals, the IRS, in the spirit of the announcement, have processed recalcitrant taxpayers without penalties and criminal prosecution. This means that on the strength of the legitimate expectations doctrine, taxpayers seeking to rely on this practice can do so with the assurance that any deviation from this practice by the IRS can be met with a court order compelling them to do so in line with their practice. Until the IRS announces the practice has changed into the future, they are bound by it.

The Media Company Business Sale

AFTER YEARS OF mergers and acquisition involving a number of media-related companies, a dominant holding company emerged. The final step involved is the sale of the main business, with a cash injection into the holding company's business. The plan was then to distribute the capital profit of the family of companies up to the ultimate holding company, where the funds were required to fund a new series of acquisitions. This meant that dividends had to be declared to the ultimate holding company. Provided that the indirect subsidiary company selling the media business and the various intermediate subsidiary companies fell within a group of company's structure, where the ultimate holding company held directly and indirectly 70% of the shares in the dividend, an election could be made to exempt each dividend declaration from tax.

Fortunately, management decided to compile a tax team to look at the transaction, just before it was to be finally implemented. It did not take the tax team long, after assessing all the relevant facts, that a problem could exist if urgent commercial steps were not taken.

The problem was that the intermediate subsidiary company did not directly or indirectly hold 70% of the ultimate holding company, because a number of minority shareholders held the balance of shares. It had always been the intention of the ultimate holding company to simplify the group structure and to buy out the minorities. No one had thought of doing this at the time that the media business was sold. Now the problem had manifested itself into one that would cost the group of companies an unnecessary dividend tax, unless a solution could be implemented, without falling foul of the antiavoidance provisions of the governing tax legislation.

The tax team needed further urgent facts of exactly what the state of play was in the main underlying transaction of the sale of the media business. On carefully working out which minority shareholders had to be bought out in the intermediate subsidiary, it became apparent that the main transaction was held up by the nonfulfillment of an approval from another regulatory authority. This was still to take a number of weeks to complete. Breathing space was found—last minute.

An intermediate transaction could be orchestrated, buying out the minorities, so as to create the group company structure (as was originally planned) with the added benefit that the dividend tax exemption could be claimed.

Finally, a small block of shares held by the ultimate holding company had to be repurchased by the intermediate company in a stock buyback transaction. The problem with this leg of this transaction was that the stock buyback could only take place on the actual registration of a special resolution with the registrar of companies. Without the actual registration of the special resolution, the share buyback would be invalid; and the 70% group of companies would not be fulfilled, no matter how carefully planned.

The fact that an outstanding suspensive condition still had to be met, plus the actual registration of a special resolution, gave effect to a very important step in the execution of the plan, which resulted in tens of millions of dollars of dividend tax being spared. Had one of these steps not been "picked up" and resolved in the normal course of a commercially motivated transaction, the transaction would have had a significant and unwarranted tax leak.

Forgetting to Clean Up Afterward

THE POSITIVE PREPLANNED result in the media business sale above, did not result in this case. A major consumer supplier decided to sell an unrelated group company for approximately $300m. The transaction was simple enough. When the business had been sold, all that had to happen was that the holding company had to be deregistered within a five-year period; and the deregistration dividend, in anticipation of the deregistration steps being taken, could be declared to the parent group, exempt of dividend tax. As simple as that!

The sale took place. The deregistration dividend was declared, exempt of dividends tax, but the company was not deregistered. Five years later, six years later, and in the seventh year as part of the TRM™ process, the mistake was uncovered in the main group of companies. How was this possible? Such a simple step!

Immediately a thorough investigation was conducted to establish from all the relevant facts how this could happen. The facts provided the answer and a way out of having to pay tens of millions of dollars dividend tax.

At the time the transaction was concluded, the responsibility of deregistering the company was left to a major international accounting firm, which ceased operating shortly after the transaction ended. All the functions they were performing were transferred to a new accounting firm. Somehow this deregistration transaction slipped through, and no one picked it up! The intention to deregister the company, however, had always been there. It was also found, through the appropriate research by the tax team, that the taxman also had a discretion to condone the late deregistration of companies on good cause shown. The good cause shown was the facts uncovered. The discretion was exercised, and the taxpayer got away with paying no dividend tax.

A simple oversight could have cost the groups as much as an extra 30% on their annual tax bill. How's that for an exposure of a significant uncovered tax risk from just one simple transaction that had gone wrong! Had proper past transaction legal audit steps been implemented as part of a broader tax risk management TRM™ strategy, the oversight would have been discovered well before the expiry of the five-year period.

In larger groups of companies the change of guard at management level often results in oversights that are this simple. Unless a documented tax risk management TRM™ strategy is in place, with the guidance of an established tax team helping the new watch to pick up where the others left off, loose ends will result in unnecessary tax revised assessments.

A Case of Skeletons in the Cupboard

THERE ARE FREQUENTLY whispers in the corridors of power: "Can you believe we did *that* transaction eight years ago? If the authorities even join all the dots, many eyebrows will be raised and some heads may roll!"

This commentary, no matter how unfounded it might appear, cannot go unnoticed by the tax team and part of a tax risk management TRM™ strategy process. Nothing is more dangerous than unsubstantiated rumors which have a habit of metamorphosing into new convoluted versions as the years tick on. Confront these transactions.

Firstly, go to the most reliable sources. Interview under legal privilege the original participants in the transaction. Access all documentary evidence. Get the most accurate actual factual version. Then, from this starting point, determine from the best facts available what the real and actual story is. So often the suspicion of "fraud" or "unlawful" is totally unfounded, burying once and for all the unfounded rumors and suspicions.

On occasion a fault may be uncovered which can then be dealt with in the normal course of the TRM™ process.

The IRS Query

THE INITIAL LETTER from the IRS will usually request from the taxpayer a list of documentation and information.

Whenever the IRS requires a taxpayer to furnish documentation and information, the IRS must state the administrative purpose for which it is sought.

All information provided must be of a factual nature; and the IRS is not entitled to information that extends to the realm of ideas, opinions, or judgments.

An example of an IRS query dealing with a transaction would typically include the following:

> Kindly furnish by [x date] a detailed reply to the following observations or inquiries arising out of an examination of the annual financial statements of your company.
>
> ➤ Factual diagrammatical flowchart highlighting all transaction and cash flows and the respective dates and the names of the parties involved.
>
> ➤ Bank statements reflecting the cash flows.
>
> ➤ Loan applications and all related correspondence.
>
> ➤ Information furnished on requesting approval of the loan facility as well as information furnished on review of the facility.
>
> ➤ All agreements, addendums, amended agreements, side letters or verbal understandings and supporting documentation. Copy of the complete synopsis or presentation regarding the structure.
>
> ➤ Name of entity marketing the structure as well as marketing person.

➤ The accounting and tax treatments including journals as well as the cash flows for all transactions already accounted for and for the transactions to be accounted for in future.

➤ Discuss the extent to which the company complied or did not comply with AC 125 Financial Instruments: Disclosure and Presentation.

➤ Reasons as to the purpose for entering into these financial agreements.

➤ All opinions obtained from lawyers, auditors or any other party relating to this transaction. If you are of the view that these opinions are subject to legal privilege, kindly support your view with detailed reasons.

➤ Copies of correspondence by the auditors with the relevant bank.

➤ Detailed opinions why you are of the view that you are entitled to the deduction.

➤ Detailed valuation report with regard to the share value of the forward purchase of shares plus working papers including a discussion of the valuation methods used.

➤ Kindly explain the consequences and remedies for all the agreements involved in the structured deal and for each of the parties involved under the following circumstances:

• If the taxpayer does not perform in terms of the agreements concluded.

• If the taxpayer is placed in liquidation.

• If the bank is placed in liquidation.

• If the taxpayer wishes to exit out of the structured deal.

The following guidelines should be considered before furnishing the IRS with any documentation and information:

❑ Make sure that no generic marketing brochures, presentations, or proposals are furnished. All relevant documentation should be tailor-made to the specific transaction.

❑ Ensure that all correspondence pertains specifically to the final structure implemented.

❑ Ensure that only final versions of the agreements, addendums, and side letters are provided.

❑ Any verbal understandings must be given by the role players and preferably recorded in affidavits.

How to Question the IRS

IN CERTAIN CIRCUMSTANCES it may become apparent that the IRS query is a "fishing expedition." The taxpayer has rights to ask the IRS what the relevance of their questions is and to clarify ambiguous requests. The taxpayer is entitled to know precisely what the administrative purpose of the query is. In this regard the taxpayer may pose questions set out in the TQQ in the "TRM™ Dictionary" at the beginning of this special report (please take note of the disclaimer at the end of the definition of TQQ at the beginning of this special report).

Obtaining the Facts

AS SOON AS the IRS query is received, a full factual inquiry should be performed by the taxpayer.

Ideally a taxpayer should preempt any IRS investigation when it comes to transactions previously concluded and start compiling and saving records as soon as possible.

Apart from the written documentation, it is important to identify the key role players involved at the time the transaction was discussed and entered into. Such role players should be interviewed. This may be necessary down the line as these role players could be called to testify as witnesses.

Interviews should preferably be conducted by your advisors as they will be proficient with the type of questions that would normally be posed.

The other reason for conducting interviews is that people's recollection of certain matters tends to diminish over time, so the sooner you can get a recordal the better and more accurate it will be. The role players inevitably resign, retire, change employment, or die. Accordingly, it is best to obtain the information while they are still employed at the relevant entity and can easily cooperate.

Interact with Financial Institutions

INVOLVE THE RELEVANT financial institution right from the start. They must be made aware, up front, that they are to advise the taxpayer of any IRS queries they receive and that any documentation and/or information they intend to furnish in response thereto must be reviewed and approved by the taxpayer before it is submitted.

Before the financial institution answers any queries, it is essential that the taxpayer receive all the records in the financial institution's possession pertaining to the transaction.

The financial institution may not see the relevance in providing the taxpayer with everything, but tax attorneys will know what is crucial to the case and what is detrimental, and it may be that certain documentation which is damaging is in fact completely irrelevant to the ultimate transaction and so should not be furnished to the IRS.

In some cases the records are stored offshore. In these circumstances it is important to insist that copies of everything are received so that the taxpayer is not put in the predicament when IRS raises a query that the records are not available.

Bringing the Financial Institution to the Party

THE FINANCIAL INSTITUTION played the main role in selling the transaction product to the taxpayer and most times assured the taxpayer that the structure was not untoward in light of expert opinions obtained. Accordingly, the financial institution should be held partially responsible for their role in devising and offering the product.

Similarly, the opinions the financial institution obtained could assist the taxpayer's case and should be disclosed to the taxpayer, who in turn may elect to provide the contents to the IRS.

Just because the financial institution sold the product to the taxpayer, it does not mean that they are no longer involved. Representatives thereof will have intimate knowledge of the transaction and why it does not fall foul of the law. Accordingly, they should assist the taxpayer in formulating counterarguments to any queries raised by the IRS.

In many cases there is a sound business rationale for including a particular step in the transaction, which should be considered from the financial institution's perspective, and not necessarily from the taxpayer's perspective. In these circumstances the taxpayer may not have knowledge of it, and it is therefore crucial to involve the financial institution in explaining the purpose in terms thereof.

Repricing Agreements

A REPRICING AGREEMENT can be in the form of a separate agreement, a clause, or an addendum; but it essentially provides for circumstances which occur or manifest later into the transaction and which impacts on the financial model of the structure, which may not have been contemplated.

Circumstances may include the introduction of and changes to any law, rule, regulation, directive, or banking practice applicable to the transaction, the rate and practice of levying tax, damages, and other costs which may become payable due to a breach. Of course there are innumerable scenarios which are not necessarily envisaged by the financial institution from the outset.

The effect of this is that such circumstance will be incorporated in the financial model which will then affect the payments made by the taxpayer under the agreements (e.g., rentals, interest, loan repayments, or any other form of payment).

Taxpayers must be vigilant when they enter into settlements with the IRS because they will invariably result in an adjustment to the model in accordance with the repricing agreement.

Aiming toward a Letter of Findings

IDEALLY THE TAXPAYER'S representatives should attempt to establish a high-level relationship with representatives from the IRS. In so doing, an introductory meeting should be convened wherein the representatives discuss the way forward and the amicable approach they intend to adopt.

This is also an important forum for the taxpayer to emphasize that a letter of findings must be issued by the IRS prior to any assessments and that the taxpayer be given reasonable opportunity to respond to the letter of findings.

The basis of the relationship is one of constant interaction so that if the IRS requires additional information and/or documentation, the IRS should request same from the taxpayer instead of arriving at inferences without first obtaining concrete evidence.

The Essence of a Transaction

THE ENTIRE TRANSACTION, and its individual parts, must be carefully scrutinized to ensure that each component is legally and properly implemented. It may be that one of the transaction legs was not implemented properly by the financial institution and is therefore invalid. This flaw, if a fundamental pillar of the transaction, could shift the liability to the financial institution, or another party that failed to execute it properly.

In summary, the taxpayer must investigate the transaction from all angles as they will be held accountable.

In recent times, it has become apparent that with the execution of a series of steps in more complex mergers and acquisitions, special resolutions are required to be registered at the company's registrar's office, of the appropriate regulator. Often this step is ignored, which means that a key step in the series of steps has not been properly executed. Unexpected and negative tax consequences may flow as a result. Double-check. Other times, taxpayers take advice from corporate advisors, change aspects of the transaction that may be key, and then make the cardinal error of not going back to the corporate advisors to double-check.

In a recent case, the corporate advisors had structured a share buyback transaction by granting the subsidiary company the option to buyback its shares from a shareholder at a fixed price in the future, after paying a price for the option now. The company secretary decided to amend the transaction without referring the detail back to the corporate advisors. The amendments to the agreements were made. Eighteen months later, when the subsidiary company needed to exercise the share buyback option, it was discovered that the wording of the agreements had been changed by the company secretary in such a way that the option and buyback had taken place simultaneously eighteen months before. The problem was that the special resolution giving effect to this transaction, although signed eighteen months before, waiting for the option to be exercised, could no longer be implemented as it should have been registered by law within six months of the resolution having been taken. The entire transaction had to be redone. Fortunately it was discovered that due to the share buyback being invalid, as the special resolution was not registered, there were no tax consequences in terms of the Companies Act. However, there had been an unlawful transgression by not registering the special resolution.

Legal Privilege

ANY OPINIONS OBTAINED from the outset, before and pursuant to an IRS query, must be protected by legal privilege. This will ensure they do not have to be disclosed to the IRS at all, even if the matter eventually goes to court.

Opinions may contain qualifications or provisos. For example, counsel may arrive at a finding on the assumption of something. If this gets into the IRS's hands, they could focus on that qualification and misinterpret it entirely.

Taxpayers must make sure to furnish counsel with every last detail in order to avoid such assumptions.

Report to the Audit Committee and a Provision Recommendation

A TAX EXPOSURE is typically a combination of capital, penalties, and interest. A determination must be made, based on the information available, as to whether there is a tax exposure or whether circumstances exist to mitigate or eliminate the exposure. Based on this determination the amount is either provided for, raised as a contingent liability, or excluded as an exposure.

In reporting to the audit committee, the tax exposure is dependent on the facts of the matter which in turn will dictate the risk. The risk could be classified into three categories, namely, probable, possible, and remote. Each category should have a corresponding percentage, e.g., 100%, 50%, and 20% respectively. This will quantify the provision to be made for each item and will give the committee a better understanding of the exposure.

In the USA, having an estimated 50% or more potential risk exposure means that FIN 48, referred to in the chapter 8, will come into play for public companies.

Chapter 6

Internal Audits Fix Financial Accounting Problems

Executive Summary

MANY BUSINESSES PUT their blind faith in reactive reporting by their auditors or accountants and expect that their tax manager through the route of normal tax compliance will resolve all tax risks. In the difficult regulatory environment that taxpayers operate in, this is not a prudent tax risk management TRM™ strategy. Businesses need to have their own internal control and check mechanisms. The tax team that has been formed will also assist in performing internal audits associated with tax risk management TRM™. They must be privy to all information, subject to legal privilege, in order to identify, analyze, and solve tax risks effectively, such as accounting provisions, for instance. The tax team, with internal audit, must be placed into a position to gain more information and impose controls and checks on a regular basis, and not only when the outside accountants conduct an audit.

Introduction

CHAPTERS 1 TO 5 have taken the tax risk management process from a proactive one through a tax team creating a TRM™ strategy and then ensuring that the tax manager gets outside input and more facts.

Chapter 6 deals with TRM™ Step 6.

Financial accounting supplies the numbers on which tax compliance is based. Simply relying on these numbers, as is usually the case with most tax managers, is not enough by a long shot. Internal audit procedures must be expanded to self-audit the higher tax risk areas in a business, so as to self-expose any mistakes and noncompliance before the IRS does. This plays back into proactive tax risk management and the avoidance of unexpected and additional tax charges that may be crippling, if driven by the IRS.

Internal Auditors

QUESTION: "WHAT ARE they doing, and what are they focusing on?" Tax is usually not high on the agenda. "Why not?" Because this area of risk is not being emphasized enough. "Why not?" The board of directors has not given it priority. The audit committee is not pushing for tax transparency, and so the BO/CFO does not have a pressure point to deal with and will cover it when it becomes a priority, usually as part of crisis management. The tax problems are what they are. If they are serious enough, they will emerge in good time, and the business can deal with the consequences at that point in time. Other priorities have been placed on the internal auditors' plates such as fraud in its various disguises. But is that enough?

Have You Read the Rest of This Special Report?

IF YOU FIND yourself at this point not knowing what the answer is, you have either turned directly to this page without reading the rest of the special report, or you have missed the point of this special report—be proactive, get internal audit to double-check the main tax risk areas, get help through a tax team to identify the tax risk areas, work according to a tax strategy document which is continuously revisited, avoid being insular and get out of the ivory tower, go and chase down all the facts to get an accurate picture of any tax problems around any major transaction. Communicate, communicate, and communicate again, get to know the business and all its facets, get internal audit involved to check again, and don't trust at face value your systems and the people who feed in the information. Check and check again!

Internal Auditors Revisited

HISTORICALLY THE PRESENCE of internal auditors in any business has made a significant contribution toward deterring the incidence of fraud in that business. Internal auditors should play a pivotal role in the TRM™ process by providing the much-needed support and expertise to continuously monitor the controls that are in place in order to pick up on any emerging tax risks. They are also skilled and experienced in identifying potential risk issues and have the know-how to properly investigate these risk issues.

The risk issues that require ongoing monitoring, identifying, and investigating are set out in chapter 8. It is also essential that there is proper interface between the internal auditors and the tax team, with a line of communication open to the BO/CFO and the audit committee, if need be. The entire interactive process with the internal auditors can also be enhanced by implementing some of the following measures:

❏ Regular meetings should be scheduled with the tax team to report on and get instructions on various areas of concern to perform internal tax audits.

❏ Work closely with the legal team and external tax advisors, collaborating and exchanging information such as findings, reports, and research.

❏ Report at the end of each process to the tax team.

❏ Ensure that the BO/CFO, with board backing, emphasizes the significant role of internal audits to uncover areas of tax risk in the business, with the appropriate budget and the cooperation of all concerned in the business.

❏ Assess the tax risk and the control put in place and their impact of the financial reporting process, evaluating the qualities of the controls and the reporting process.

❏ Monitor compliance by the business sectors with the TRM™ strategy devised by the tax team.

Collusion

IN A NUMBER of cases, personnel will take advantage of a tax risk weakness to give a benefit in favor of a connected person to the potential detriment of the business. In the absence of strict internal auditing being performed in the area of payroll taxes, opportunities abound for personnel to apply lax standards to taxing benefits or perks granted to certain employees. In other areas, independent contractors will be granted favorable terms, with the minimum deduction or no deduction of payroll taxes, to their benefit, but to the detriment of the business. If any discrepancy arises, the IRS will look to the business to make good any shortfall.

This type of collision can be avoided by communicating to the personnel and payroll departments that thorough and frequent internal audits should be conducted.

Management Override of Controls

MANAGEMENT MAY FROM time to time override controls put into place to ensure proper corporate governance. This usually happens with nonrecurring or nonstandard transactions or events. But this in turn leads to an override of established policies and procedures, usually with the intention of enhancing the business's financial situation. Any such transgressions must be prohibited, unless with the approval of the board of directors, who should be made aware of the potential consequences.

This type of transgression in tax compliance takes place every month in most businesses when secured data is extracted from systems such as SAP or an equivalent Oracle database and dumped into a spreadsheet to manipulate for the purposes of compiling and analyzing data to complete tax returns. The spreadsheets are unsecure, and the propensity for the data to be corrupted is ever present. It is that simple. Extract the financial data from the business SAP system into a spreadsheet that is not tamper proof. If the responsible person did not build the spreadsheet and is working off a previously used template, expect mistakes. Who will ultimately check the accuracy of the information being manipulated in the spreadsheet? Usually no one.

This special report override of controls can be combated through communicating to all concerned that these practices must cease immediately, and resources must be provided for an alternate method.

Compiling the Tax Pack

THE TAX MANAGER will usually receive the basic components of the tax pack from the various financial managers in the various divisions of the business. The purpose behind this step is for each financial manager to review the financial accounting treatment of various accruals for accounting purposes and deductions for accounting purposes, so as to determine what accrual and deduction adjustments must be made for tax purposes in compiling the tax return for that year of assessment. Simple enough?

A tax manager of a major international consumer product multinational decided to review a few of the most recent tax packs. He found some interesting and consistent mistakes made by most of the financial managers preparing the tax pack information. Expenses they wanted to disallow for tax purposes were all for marketing purposes and were clearly deductible, but they had been marked not deductible, because certain employees who enjoyed these benefits had not been subjected to perks tax. The two concepts are completely different, and there was no reason to not deduct the expenses albeit the need to look at the perks received by the employees.

Provisions and Tax

WHEN BUSINESSES ACQUIRE database management and tracking systems such as SAP- or Oracle-based systems, closing balances from the previous systems used are transferred as opening balances to the new system.

After a number of years, and a change of guard at management level, the understanding and specific knowledge required to determine how those opening balances were made up. The old closing balance records are destroyed or get lost.

If a specific inquiry is directed at these opening balances, many businesses have problems in providing the detail. A common problem.

The problem is about to get worse. Many accounting provisions are not allowed as deductible tax expenses until the actual expense or loss provided for actually occurs in the tax year in question. It happens that these provisions created by previous BO/CFOs and transferred from old to new systems may end up getting a life of their own as tax-deductible expenses, which should not be claimed. A blatant tax-deduction error.

What tax provisions may create these problems? The problem children are

❑ postretirement funding provisions,

❑ maintenance provisions,

❑ bonus provisions,

❑ obsolete stock provisions,

❑ price variance provisions,

❑ doubtful debt provisions,

❑ credit note provisions,

❑ returnable container provisions, and

❑ early settlement discounts.

Chapter 7

Communication to Eliminate Tax Risk

> The SEC in USA's chief accountant said, "Sunlight is said to be one of the best disinfectants, and the area of income tax accounting could use more sunlight."

Executive Summary

COMMUNICATION IS VITAL to the entire tax risk management TRM™ process. Effective communication channels must be opened up and maintained on a regular basis, especially with the operations divisions of a business where there is often the least amount of transparent communication with the tax manager. Internal meetings between the various departments and the tax team must be encouraged on a more regular basis where all potential risk areas must be divulged to the tax team. Informal communication channels must also be present and allow all the various departments within a business access to the tax team should they need it.

Effective interaction and sharing of information with a person within the IRS must also be seen as important. Creating and maintaining an effective and amicable relationship allows you to have one foot in the door at the IRS.

Effective communication will allow the business to be well prepared when the IRS is to conduct tax compliance audits from time to time.

Introduction

THIS IS THE last, but not least important, TRM™ Step 7.

The previous six chapters flowing from proactive tax risk management, with the tax team, compiling a TRM™ strategy, getting to a point of embracing transparency and outside assistance, to obtaining more facts, and then ensuring internal audits verify the correctness of tax compliance, brings the TRM™ process finally to the common golden thread that binds all these chapters and their processes together—communication!

Lack of communication between the tax manager and the rest of the business, and only processing numbers to compile tax returns, is the reason why tax compliance in most businesses only covers 40% of the total tax risk in those businesses. The other 60% tax risk is hidden and can only be exposed through a systematic process of people-to-people communication, and not just through processing numbers. The one must verify the other. This calls for new communication systems to be implemented in the business to circumvent and put an end to the bad habit of limited people communication.

Missed Communication

THE LEADING CHARACTERS in this special report have been business owners, the BO/CFO, the tax manager, and the legal team. Much has been written about the formation of the tax team and the interaction with the outside advisors and other key participants. Hell, even communication with the CEO, the board, and the audit committee has been suggested. Why then a chapter dedicated to communication to eliminate operations tax risk?

The fact is that historically in-house tax compliance departments have formed part of an ivory tower comprised of senior management, where communication is limited. In many instances the tax compliance function has been outsourced to outside tax consultants, who are definitely not in touch with the day-to-day business operations. They rely on financial accounting information to compile tax compliance documents.

Throughout the TRM™ process, it will become apparent how important person-to-person communication between members of the tax team is, leading to the exposure of off-the-radar screen issues that may otherwise never have occurred prior to an IRS audit. Communicating with people is key. Communicating with numbers alone is not.

Numbers Get You into Trouble

TAKE THE CASE of Equinox Ltd. (a fictitious name for the real company). It had garnered up thousands of VAT input tax credit invoices, with which it had claimed millions of dollars worth of input tax credits. The VAT legislation required Equinox Ltd. to ensure that the VAT number of suppliers was on all tax invoices. This also meant that the VAT number had to be correct.

After a while, the IRS conducted a VAT audit and reviewed a batch of tax invoices for a specified period. It became obvious quite quickly that all the tax invoices from one particular supplier in the review period were invalid. The VAT number of the supplier was incorrect. In fact, the supplier had fraudulently given the wrong VAT number—a fictitious one. As a result the IRS pulled all the tax invoices given by that supplier. All the VAT numbers were wrong, and all the tax invoices were invalid for claiming input tax credits. All the previously claimed input tax credits were added back in a revised assessment, plus penalties and interest. The end assessment totaled up a considerable sum in dollars.

Equinox Ltd. had not got to know its supplier properly—so it seemed. On a deeper analysis, it became apparent that the general manager of the operating division in question had terminated the supply relationship with the supplier in question, under suspicious circumstances. Another supplier replaced the dodgy supplier in question, but no communication had taken place between the tax manager and the general manager. There was no facility in place for this to happen. Besides what more had to be said? The supplier had been replaced, and no apparent harm seemed to have been suffered by Equinox Ltd.

Had any competent tax manager been made aware of the suspicious circumstances around the termination of the relationship with the supplier, they would most likely had double-checked all relevant information at hand of the supplier to ensure that it was correct. Had a self-discovery been made of the false VAT number, criminal charges could have been pursued. The IRS voluntarily approached Equinox Ltd. as they had been on the receiving end of a fraud. A soft outcomes result could have been negotiated with full cooperation between the two to see the perpetrator paying for its fraud. Instead, the IRS, as it always does, goes for the soft target, i.e., Equinox Ltd. or its equivalent.

If a regulated and regular communication system existed between the tax manager and the operations division, the negative tax consequences would have been averted.

Human Judgment under Pressure

HUMAN JUDGMENT, ESPECIALLY when subjected to pressure, is imperfect. Unless checks and balances are introduced, and encouragement exists to communicate pressurized decisions that may have a negative tax implication, improper human judgment will lead to additional tax risk. For instance, it often happens in a merger acquisition scenario that parties to the transaction are placed under great pressure. Deadlines are created, and parties from all sides do their absolute best to ensure that the deadline is met, for fear of reprisals that may stem from causing the merger or acquisition to flounder.

Level-headed thinking by management, albeit at the eleventh hour, caused the professional members of the tax team to be introduced to giving last-minute guidance on the transaction about to take place in the media company business sale case study mentioned in chapter 5.

In order to discourage human judgment error, encourage open channels of communication so that personnel under pressure can seek guidance and assistance on demand.

Breakdown of Communication

PERSONNEL OFTEN MISUNDERSTAND instructions or make mistakes due to overwork, carelessness, or distraction. Temporary or new personnel may also not be adequately trained on new processes they have been introduced to. All of which contributes to the creation of additional unnecessary risks.

Breakdown can be avoided by careful and consistent communication, especially to new and temporary personnel.

Innermetrix©

IN THE PROCESS of implementing the tax risk management TRM™ system, in order to minimize tax risk on an ongoing basis, it will be necessary to implement a communication system between the tax compliance division, the financial accounting divisions, the transaction division, and the operations of the business. The communication process will require frequent documentation, which attempts to highlight any tax risk that has developed in each of the mentioned divisions, to the tax compliance division, through a systematic series of questionnaires generated by the tax compliance division.

The reliability of the information gathered from key personnel, in the various divisions by means of these questionnaires, will depend on the integrity of those key individuals which can be measured by paying attention to a number of personality traits of each individual:

❏ attitude to compliance

❏ attention to detail

❏ following directions

❑ respect for policies

❑ role awareness

❑ practical thinking

❑ consistency and reliability

❑ meeting standards

❑ personal accountability

❑ systems judgment

These subjective factors can be measured in each individual participating in the tax risk management TRM™ system by putting them through the Innermetrix© process which takes each individual no more than fifteen minutes to complete. This process will provide the BO/CFO and tax manager with a report setting out the relevant strengths and weaknesses of each individual who participates in answering the questionnaires, in a procedure designed to maximize accuracy and limit the manifestation of the material weaknesses that regulatory authorities, like the IRS, are permanently trying to eradicate.

For instance, if an individual scores high on a majority of these subjective indicators, there is an assurance that he or she will take the process seriously and give accurate and complete information on a regular basis. If the score shows a weakness in a number of these subjective indicators, then management will have the opportunity through an initial training process to emphasize the significance of accurate and complete information, and they will also know which questionnaires that have been submitted to them need to be scrutinized with greater care to ensure that the participant has completed his or her task properly.

For example, if a participant shows a weakness in many areas, the tax manager would always telephone that individual after the completion of each questionnaire to discuss the answers given. In this way the tax manager can ensure that the proper attention had been given to the questionnaire by that individual.

Through this management process the individuals showing any weaknesses will usually, through a process of interaction and teaching, improve those weaknesses and as such become more reliable in the information that they provide.

The Innermetrix© testing will be repeated six monthly so as to keep monitoring any changes in the strengths and weaknesses of these personality traits. The test can be accessed at www.innermetrix.com.

The Communication Questions

THE QUESTIONS PUT to the operations divisions in the business that will require regular review, as part of the TRM™ strategy, will include the following:

❑ Do you know which perks or fringe benefits are subject to VAT?

❑ Have you accounted for VAT on any perks or fringe benefits?

❑ Have you exported any goods or services?

❑ Have you imported any software over the Internet and accounted for the VAT?

❑ Are your export documents 100% compliant with the tax regulations? Have you actually checked? Where are the documents kept?

❑ How accurate are your invoices for claiming VAT input tax credits? Have you double-checked that the supplier vendor VAT numbers are correct?

❑ Have you paid any reimbursements to employees over the last period?

❑ Have you created, transferred balances, or created any accounting provisions? What are they?

❑ Have you accounted for any doubtful or bad debt write-offs?

❑ Do you meet regularly with your BO/CFO or tax manager to discuss any potential tax risks?

❑ Have you created, exercised, or disposed of any options?

❑ Do you have any low-cost assets that could be written off for tax purposes in the current year of assessment?

❑ Have you acquired or disposed of any assets, or do you intend to do so in the next quarter?

❑ Will any of the above disposals or acquisitions require any permission or registration with a federal or government department?

❑ Have you conducted an internal audit, including a review of tax risk areas, in the last twelve months?

❑ Do you have any outstanding IRS inquiries?

❑ Have you done an Innermetrix© profile in the last six months?

These questions should also be put to the transactions and financial accounting sectors of the business from time to time, to answer and review the answers given by the operations managers. In this manner, consistency in the business toward tax triggers in the business can be constantly monitored.

Results should also be analyzed by the tax team and reported to the audit committee from time to time.

This type of detail will not be necessary for small businesses that have entered the tax-Radar™ program.

The execution of this process for a large corporation is best undertaken through an adaptation or extension to the IT intranet set up for the business to facilitate any IT-driven interaction between employees in the business. Any such intranet system, facilitating the transfer and exchange of tax information or related information, should be made with the appropriate security structure in place to ensure secrecy and confidentiality at all times, with overall access only limited to the CEO, BO/CFO, and tax manager. Such a system can also record the ongoing tax issues in the business. The design of such a system is set out in appendix 5.

TRM™ Web Interface System—V1.01

The purpose of this IT specification of a Tax Risk Management Web Interface System (phew! a mouthful of IT jargon, but simply put as the "TRM™ Web Interface") is to determine an organization's tax risk and from that point forward to help manage that tax risk. The TRM™ Web Interface is one of the key TRM™ tools used.

The following aspects are important in the execution of TRM™ Web Interface:

❑ Security—TRM™ Web Interface security is key. The information housed in the system is very sensitive and can only be viewed by preselected persons. For this reason the following security measures are vital:

○ Secure log-in system.

○ SSL encryption from point of log-in.

○ Secure database environment.

○ Secure remote hosting facility.

○ File locking facility.

❑ Intended audience—TRM™ Web Interface will be made available to the tax team (including the tax manager and the BO/CFO) and the CEO.

❑ Hosting—So as to ensure legal privilege, the TRM™ Web Interface should be hosted in a secure remote facility controlled and under the supervision of the legal team, with access via the Internet using SSL encryption.

❑ Database—The database needs to be scalable and secure.

❑ Interface—This is Web based. Easy navigation is important that most people using the facility can identify with and are used to operating on.

❑ Third-party media—The standard word processing and spreadsheet documents are required to be viewed through the system, with rights only given to key people to edit these documents. The uploading of these files need to be secure to avoid any tampering with the documents.

❑ Tax returns details are to be published.

The TRM™ Web Interface design should entail some of the following features:

❑ Interface customization according to each division in the business to be separately identifiable, with a consolidation option.

❑ Log on through a three-level log-on secure method:

○ Username

○ PIN code with five digits

○ Individually selected password

❑ Dashboard, being the landing page, where once a browser has logged onto the system, it will display all the critical information that is important to view at a glance, with the following sections:

○ A **notice board** that can be changed by select users to make announcements

○ **Work in Progress** ("WIP") showing any tax compliance issues that must be attended to in the next thirty days

○ **Work completed** in the last thirty days

○ The **tax team diary** and agenda for each forthcoming meeting

○ **On-the-radar screen** issues, with each one quantified with a risk weighting attached to the estimate

○ **Off-the-radar screen** issues, with each one quantified with a risk weighting attached to the estimate

○ **Tax planning** issues identified, with each one quantified with a risk weighting attached to the estimate

Notice Board

This is a simple notice area, displaying relevant information to those who are using the system. It requires the following fields:

○ Date posted

○ Person who posted notice

○ Detail of notice

Work in Progress

Work in progress defines the work currently being done on any tax return within the organization. This is put into place in order to ensure that every single tax return is completed timeously and as accurately as possible, using the defined guidelines proposed by the tax team. A return will appear in the work in progress as soon as it is received from the IRS and added to the system.

The data required for the WIP section is as follows:

❏ Date received

❑ Due date

❑ Project manager (linking to users, with all contact Information)

❑ Operator (person whose task has been assigned to—linking to users, with all contact Information)

❑ Project status (percentage complete)

❑ Preparation schedule (PDF)—this is the supporting document, explaining what is to be submitted in the tax return

❑ Tax return (PDF)—this is to be updated as the return is completed

❑ IRS guideline (PDF)—this is the IRS guideline for the completion of the return

❑ Preparation guideline (PDF)—this will be a general document defined by the tax team for the processing of such tax returns. Each different tax will have its own guideline.

❑ WIP comments—The project manager and operator is required to enter comments throughout the process. These comments include

○ date submitted,

○ comment body,

○ person who posted comment, and

○ date tax return was submitted to the IRS.

Other key dates that may be required in the management process are

❑ date of prescription,

❑ date of query letter from the IRS,

❑ date query response due to the IRS, and

❑ date reply to response due from the IRS.

WIP Work Flow Process

The WIP work flow process is important as this defines how and what is done in order to ensure that the returns are submitted in time.

❑ Receive the IRS return.

❑ Return added to the TRM™ Web Interface in PDF format.

❑ Entry created in WIP.

❑ Project manager assigns operator.

❑ E-mail sent to all members of the tax team notifying them of the receipt of the IRS return, due date, and people responsible for completing tax return.

❑ Thirty days prior to return due date entry is added to the WIP area on the "Switchboard."

❑ Thirty days prior to return due date an e-mail sent to all members of the tax team notifying them of status (the e-mail displays return receipt date, due date, and people responsible within the organization).

❑ One week prior to return due date entry is marked RED (CRITICAL) on the WIP area on the "Switchboard."

❑ One week prior to return due date a CRITICAL e-mail sent to all members of the tax team notifying them of status (the e-mail displays return receipt date, due date, and people responsible within the organization). From this point an e-mail is sent daily to each member of the committee until the due date.

❑ If the return is not submitted marked for send-off on the due date the return is automatically added to the on-the-radar screen tax issues.

❑ An e-mail is sent to each member of the tax team notifying them that the due date has been missed. An e-mail is sent daily informing each member of the status.

When the return is submitted it is automatically removed from WIP and placed in Work Completed.

Work Completed

Work completed shows all returns that have been successfully submitted. Information that is important here is the following:

❑ Date received

❑ Due date

❑ Project manager (linking to users, with all contact information)

❑ Operator (person whose task has been assigned to—linking to Users, with all contact information)

❑ Preparation schedule (PDF)—this is the supporting document, explaining what is to be submitted in the tax return

❑ Tax return (PDF)—this is to be updated as the return is completed

❑ IRS Guideline (PDF)—this is the IRS guideline for the completion of the return

❑ Preparation guideline (PDF)—this will be a general document defined by the tax team for the processing of such tax returns. Each different tax will have its own guideline.

❑ WIP comments—The project manager and operator are required to enter comments throughout the process. These comments include

○ date submitted,

○ comment body,

○ person who posted comment, and

○ date tax return was submitted to the IRS.

Other key dates that may be required in the management process are

❑ date of prescription,

❑ date of query letter from the IRS,

❑ date query response due to the IRS, and

❑ date reply to response due from the IRS.

Work Completed Work Flow

Work completed work flow is as follows:

❑ On submission of return the WIP item is automatically added to the "Work Completed" section.

❑ An e-mail is sent notifying each member of the tax risk committee of the submission of the return.

❑ For thirty days after the submission the entry is displayed in "Work Completed" area on the "Switchboard."

❑ Thirty days after the submission the entry is removed from the "Switchboard" but is still available to view in the "Work Completed" section.

Tax Team Diary

The diary acts as a notice board, notifying the members of the tax team of the next meeting. The tax manager is responsible for the submission of information.

The data displayed is as follows:

- ❑ Meeting date

- ❑ Meeting time

- ❑ Meeting venue

- ❑ People to attend

- ❑ Discussion points

- ❑ Facility to upload complete agenda

- ❑ Facility to add to agenda (by each member of the tax team)

Work Flow

- ❑ On submission of diary event an e-mail is sent to each member of the tax team notifying them of such an event.

- ❑ The "Switchboard" displays the NEXT tax team meeting.

- ❑ A notification e-mail is sent to each member one month prior to meeting.

- ❑ A notification e-mail is sent to each member one week prior to meeting.

- ❑ A notification e-mail is sent to each member two days prior to meeting.

- ❑ A notification e-mail is sent to each member one day prior to meeting.

- ❑ Diary entry is automatically removed from "Switchboard" at time of meeting, and if the next date is already added this will be displayed.

On-the-Radar Screen Issues

This is one of the key areas. This displays all tasks that have been identified by the tax team as risk areas within the organization and are known to the IRS. These risks have been quantified, and a total value of the overall tax risk exposure is displayed.

Off-the-Radar Screen Issues

This is another key area. This displays all tasks that have been identified by the tax team but not known by the IRS. These risks have been quantified, and a total value of the overall tax risk exposure is displayed.

Tax Planning

Once a tax risk has been resolved it becomes a potential opportunity for tax planning. This section quantifies each tax planning project, showing an overall tax planning value as well as the completion status.

For additional information on the development of the TRM™ Web Interface, and to access useful templates, look at www.7taxrisks.com.

Communication and Beyond Tax Risk Management

IN AN ATTEMPT to address the occurrence of material weaknesses under SOX 404 (dealt with in chapter 8), and in an attempt to limit these exposures, Margaret S. Thomas CPA in her lecture notes on "Sarbanes-Oxley 404: Compliance and Beyond," 2006 states that "an ethical cultural environment should be created in any business. Management should create policies that create a positive environment for employees, without fear of reprisal, to report unusual occurrences. All incidents of alleged fraud or discrepancies must be investigated promptly and action taken. Employees must be encouraged to come forward with any information that may have an impact on the business."

Another area of risk is the failure of having frequent and timely meetings with the BO/CFO and the tax manager, internal auditors, and external auditors. The audit committee should meet privately with the BO/CFO, as well as with internal and external auditors to discuss the reasonableness of the reporting process, system of internal controls, tax risk, and other areas of potential concern.

In her notes Thomas goes on to share some of the following techniques that businesses can employ to ensure full compliance with compliance provisions such as SOX 404, which reiterate the processes that businesses should follow in any TRM™ process:

❑ The board and audit committee regularly discusses the effectiveness of internal controls over financial reporting, accounting policies, and procedures, including tax risk management TRM™.

❑ The board of directors reviews financial statements before they are released.

❑ The board or audit committee monitors information from anonymous reporting vehicles.

❑ The board and audit committee allocates time for discussion of issues without management present.

❑ The audit committee has at least three independent members.

❑ Internal control objectives, including information on tax risk management TRM™, and their importance, are communicated by e-mail or voice mail, regular conference calls, or Web casts.

❑ The company maintains an intranet site and posts information regarding internal controls and tax risk management TRM™.

❑ The company provides summaries of laws and regulations affecting internal controls and tax risk management TRM™.

❑ There is a direct line of communication with senior management either by e-mail or an open-door policy.

Chapter 8

The Protectors for Big Business

Introducing the Protectors

THE TERMINOLOGY MAKES one think of these acronyms as famous sporting teams. But as famous sporting teams command attention, so do these regulations insofar as they impact on tax risk. What follows is a brief summary of these regulations, their impact on tax risk management, and why an orchestrated TRM™ process will help with overall regulatory compliance.

SOX 404

THE SARBANES-OXLEY ACT was promulgated in the USA on July 30, 2002, primarily in response to the major corporate and accounting scandals in the USA such as Enron, Tyco International, Peregrine Systems, and WorldCom. Sarbanes-Oxley (also known as SOX or Sarbox) was promulgated to restore investor confidence in the reliability of the information provided by companies trading their stocks on USA stock exchanges.

SOX 404, which is an acronym for Sarbanes-Oxley Act, 2002 section 404, states,

> SEC. 404. MANAGEMENT ASSESSMENT OF INTERNAL CONTROLS.
>
> (a) RULES REQUIRED.—The Commission shall prescribe rules requiring each annual report required by section 13(a) or

15(d) of the Securities Exchange Act of 1934 (15 U.S.C. 78m or 78o(d)) to contain an internal control report, which shall—

(1) state the responsibility of management for establishing and maintaining an adequate internal control structure and procedures for financial reporting; and

(2) contain an assessment, as of the end of the most recent fiscal year of the issuer, of the effectiveness of **the internal control structure and procedures of the issuer for financial reporting**.

(b) INTERNAL CONTROL EVALUATION AND REPORTING.—With respect to the internal control assessment required by subsection (a), each registered public accounting firm that prepares or issues the audit report for the issuer shall attest to, and report on, the assessment made by the management of the issuer. An attestation made under this subsection shall be made in accordance with standards for attestation engagements issued or adopted by the Board. Any such attestation shall not be the subject of a separate engagement.

As a result of this loaded piece of legislation, areas of known or suspected weaknesses in publicly listed companies on USA stock markets must pay attention to the requirement that proper control structures and procedures on financial reporting must be put into place. This calls for the implementation of control and evaluation systems and procedures to check and double-check that the financial reporting done by these companies in every material respect is accurate, to ensure that there are no hidden surprises for investors. Any material weaknesses must, in the execution of SOX 404, be reported to the United States Securities and Exchange Commission (SEC).

It goes without saying that if up to 60% of tax risk in a business is usually hidden from the tax manager, unless a TRM™ process has been entered into to ensure that the internal control structures and procedures on the financial reporting of tax is carefully checked, material weaknesses in tax issues will result. An online company performing a market intelligence research service in the USA, in a report prepared analyzing material weaknesses in public companies since the inception of SOX 404 until May 15, 2005, reported that nearly 30% of the deficiencies were associated with tax accounting. That is significant. This also accounted for the highest deficiency under SOX 404.

The sting in the tail of SOX 404 comes in SOX 906 which prescribes the penalties corporate officers will face for noncompliance. Penalties are up to a fine of $5m and prison sentences of up to twenty years.

If the "effectiveness of **the internal control structure and procedures of the issuer for financial reporting**" has not been carefully audited, which includes the proper assessment of the tax risks in a corporation, the corporate officers may face the severe penalties mentioned above. So apart from up to six times more tax exposure by not self-regulating and self-disclosing any tax discrepancies found during a TRM™ process, the injury is further insulted in the USA with the SOX 906 penalties against corporate officers.

Auditing Standard No. 5 of the Public Company Accounting Oversight Board (PCAOB), which superseded Auditing Standard No. 2, has the following key requirements for the external auditor to consider in the process on conducting a SOX 404 review:

❑ Assess both the design and operating effectiveness of selected internal controls related to significant accounts and relevant assertions, in the context of material misstatement risks.

❑ Understand the flow of transactions, including IT aspects, sufficiently to identify points at which a misstatement could arise.

❑ Evaluate company-level (entity-level) controls, which correspond to the components of an accepted framework standard.

❑ Perform a fraud risk assessment.

❑ Evaluate controls designed to prevent or detect fraud, including management override of controls.

❑ Evaluate controls over the period-end financial reporting process.

❏ Scale the assessment based on the size and complexity of the company.

❏ Rely on management's work based on factors such as competency, objectivity, and risk.

❏ Evaluate controls over the safeguarding of assets.

❏ Conclude on the adequacy of internal control over financial reporting.

Need the BO/CFO and tax manager require more convincing where their corporation shares are trading on a USA stock exchange?

Toward this compliance, management will have to design and implement internal control and procedures that will have to be constantly monitored and audited. They will have to accept responsibility for the effectiveness of these internal controls, using suitable control criteria, supported by sufficient evidence, documentation, and a written assessment of the business's internal controls over financial reporting, in respect of the business's most recent financial year. This will include a significant module on the assessment of the business's tax position.

To comply with SOX 404, there are three basic risk types to assess and monitor:

❏ Operations

❏ Compliance with various regulatory laws

❏ Financial reporting

These requirements compare to the requirements mentioned in the rest of the special report to cover key tax risk areas in any business.

The thing about a SOX 404 process that goes into the effectiveness of a business's internal controls over financial reporting is that material weaknesses must be disclosed to the SEC, and if there is one or more material weakness, management is not permitted to conclude that its internal controls are effective. This will have repercussions in the investment arena; and apart from the SEC reporting requirement, if the material weakness is a tax-related issue, additional consequences will flow under the FIN 48 requirements, which in turn will draw the attention of the IRS.

In a sense, businesses subject to SOX 404 are really forced to conduct a tax risk management TRM™ strategy, particularly if one considers that in practice many material weaknesses reported to the SEC under SOX 404 are tax related.

Material weakness in the context of SOX 404 means a significant deficiency that, by itself, or in combination with other significant deficiencies, may result in more than a remote likelihood that a material misstatement of the financial statements will not be prevented or detected.

By way of concluding remarks, in a study done by Deloitte, the following threats to compliance have become evident in working with various businesses, giving rise to SOX 404-related concerns:

❑ lack of a business-wide executive-driven internal control management program

❑ lack of a formal business risk management program

❑ inadequate controls associated with the recording on nonroutine, complex, and unusual transactions

❑ ineffective controlled postmerger integration

❑ lack of effective controls over the IT environment

❑ ineffective financial reporting and disclosure preparation processes

❑ lack of formal controls over the financial closing process

❑ lack of current, consistent, complete, and documented accounting policies and procedures

❑ inability to evaluate and test controls over outsourced processes

❑ inadequate board and audit committee understanding of control risk

FIN 48

THE FINANCIAL ACCOUNTING Standards Board (FASB) on July 13, 2006, issued the final interpretation amending FASB Statement of Financial Accounting Standards No. 109, "Accounting for Income Taxes." Of great importance was FASB Interpretation No. 48, "Accounting for Uncertainty in Income Taxes" (FIN 48). The purpose behind publishing the interpretations was to address the uncertainty in accounting for income tax assets and liabilities. FASB No. 109, in the past, contained no guidance on accounting for income tax assets and liabilities, resulting in businesses taking inconsistent positions. According to commentators on FIN 48 at a conference of international tax practitioners in Miami during December 2006, "FIN 48 is an attempt to reconcile the inconsistencies by prescribing a consistent recognition threshold and measurement of tax assets and liabilities. It also gives taxpayers a clearly defined set of criteria to use when recognizing and measuring uncertain tax situations for financial statements, as well as specifying additional disclosures regarding the uncertainty."

The evaluation of a tax situation for FIN 48 purposes is based on a two-step process:

❑ The first step is recognition: the business determines whether it is more likely than not (which is a 50% or greater likelihood) that a tax situation would be upheld on examination, including resolution of any ensuing litigation process, based on the technical merits of the tax situation.

❑ The second step is measurement: the tax situation that meets the more-likely-than-not recognition threshold is measured to determine the amount of benefit to recognize on financial statements.

In asserting the more-likely-than-not standard, all the facts and circumstances are taken into account. Additionally, the taxpayer must presume that the tax situation will be examined by the IRS with full knowledge of all the facts, technical merits of the relevant tax law, and their applicability to the facts and circumstances of the tax situation. The taxpayer may take into account any past administrative practices and precedents of the IRS in its dealings with the business, when those practices and precedents are widely understood. Finally, each tax situation must be evaluated without consideration of the possibility of offset or addition to other tax issues.

The appropriate timing of claiming the benefits of a tax issue is when it becomes clear that the tax issue has a more-likely-than-not chance of being upheld. If a previous tax issue does not meet the more-likely-than-not standard, then it shall be adjusted in the first period after the effective date of FIN 48 (January 1, 2007).

A business must classify the liability associated with an unrecognized tax issue as a current liability to the extent the business anticipates payment of cash within one year or the operating cycle, if longer. The liability for an unrecognized tax issue shall not be combined with deferred tax liabilities or assets.

In addition to taking into account the benefit that a particular tax issue will create for a particular business, interest and penalties must also be computed in addition to the tax liability, where required by the relevant tax legislation. A tax liability will cease to be a liability during the first interim period in which any one of the following three requirements exist:

❑ The more-likely-than-not recognition threshold is met by the reporting date.

❑ The tax issue is settled through negotiation or litigation, which is where the TRM™ process plays a key role in assisting in arriving at this position where there is a problem.

❑ The statue of limitations for the IRS (prescription) to examine a tax issue has expired, unless there has been a fraud, misrepresentation, or nondisclosure by the taxpayer.

The advent of FIN 48, like SOX 404, underpins the requirement for businesses to embark upon a systematic TRM™ process to limit and expose, with the view to efficiently minimizing the incumbent risks of tax.

IFRS does exactly the same.

IFRS

THIS ACRONYM STANDS for the International Financial Reporting Standards being the standards and interpretations adopted by the International Accounting Standards Board (IASB).

During February 2006 the FASB and the IASB concluded a memorandum of understanding stating their intention to seek a convergence of their standards and interpretations by 2008. Remember FIN 48 is a FASB standard.

The effect of this is that those companies which must comply with IFRS will find that the standards expressed in FIN 48 will most probably emerge in the convergence. One of the convergence projects between the FASB and IASB is income tax.

If those companies affected by IFRS do not know what their tax risks are, need more be said about the potential problems which they will face. Read the special report again!

Remarks That Are Dynamic

> *"Strong lives are motivated by dynamic purposes."*
>
> Source: Kenneth Hildebrand

DYNAMIC MEANS "CHANGING; action and in motion."
Dynamic is synonymous with lively, active, energetic, vigorous, and impelling.
In a blink, there is more change.
In another blink, there is additional action.
In a further blink there is increasing motion.
No constant position exists in the dynamic environment of tax and tax risk management TRM™.
It is always dynamic.
The only constant is change in tax risk management TRM™.
Hence, the content of this special report is dynamic and subject to change, action, and motion.

BO/CFOs, tax managers, their boards, and audit committees are also well advised to be dynamic in their approach to a TRM™ process.
But start with being proactive.
Then embrace the constant changes.
Embark upon a continuous TRM™ process.
Then see the results of proper TRM™ management.

Once It Is All Over

THAT'S A MYTH if you understood the content of the previous section. It's never over for as long as the business has life in it. Tax risk management TRM™ will always exist to manage the continuous ebb and flow of tax issues, as the legislation changes, as the business shrinks and expands, and as the business trades continuously, with the financial results having to be documented to give account of what has happened in the previous financial year.

Chapter 9

Tax-Radar™

Visit www.tax-Radar.com for copies of the Appendices and Reports.

TRM™ Step 1—Proactive

Make the decision to take control of tax risk in your business, and know if the IRS ever pays you a visit you will have little to worry about.

Step required from you the business owner:

Are you committed to being tax risk proactive yes/no

_____ _____

             Sign   Date

TRM™ Step 2—Tax Team with tax-Radar™

Much in this special report has been dedicated to the process of forming a tax team to represent your tax interests fully. To hire a good tax manager will cost you $80,000 per year. To hire your accountants and a legal team to compile a tax review will cost you at least $50,000. To get your tax team to represent you in any tax controversy with the IRS will cost you a minimum of $65,000.

If you enter into the tax-Radar™ program for a monthly commitment of $300 through your accounting firm the Tax Risk Matrix function and any tax controversy representation with the IRS is taken care of at no additional cost to you.

Step required from you the business owner:

Complete and sign the tax-Radar™ mandate yes/no

_____   _____
            Sign   Date

See appendix 1 for the tax-Radar™ at www.tax-Radar.com to be completed and signed yes/no

_____   _____
            Sign   Date

TRM™ Step 3—Tax Risk Matrix

Once you have signed up for the tax-Radar™ program you will be expected to complete the Tax Risk Matrix with your accountant.

The Tax Risk Matrix must be kept up to date every three months.

Step required from you the business owner:

Complete and sign the Tax Risk Matrix yes/no

_____ _____
Sign   Date

See appendix 2 Tax Risk Matrix template at www.tax-Radar.com for completion yes/no

_____ _____
Sign   Date

Also see Tax Risk TRM™ Policies and Procedures Special Report at www.tax-Radar.com. Have you read this yes/no

_____ _____
Sign   Date

TRM™ Step 4—Transparency

It is important that you communicate through the Tax Risk Matrix process with your accountant every three months to keep the list of tax risks up to date. This will take a small additional commitment from you in addition to you simply expecting your accountant to complete tax compliance forms every month. You must take a keen interest in questioning what tax risks may be emerging in your business.

Step required from you the business owner:

Have you made sure that you have accessed all relevant facts to ensure your Tax Risk Matrix is complete yes/no

_____   _____
                  Sign   Date

See appendix 4 for the TRM™ Tax Risk Review Template at www.tax-Radar. com. Have you compiled a Tax Risk Review Report yes/no

TRM™ Step 5—Facts

At the time that you complete the Tax Risk Matrix you will be expected to question all key personnel in your business in compiling a complete TRM™ Tax Review Report based on the one in Appendix 4: TRM™ Tax Risk Review Template at www.tax-Radar.com.

On a three monthly basis you will be expected to spend a small amount of time with your accountant keeping your Tax Risk Matrix up to date.

Step required from you the business owner:

Have you made sure that have accessed all relevant facts after the completion of the Tax Risk Matrix, every month to make sure that the Tax Risk Matrix is kept fully up to date yes/no

_____   _____

Sign   Date

TRM™ Step 6—Fix Accounting

Any historical accounting problems must be looked at carefully to establish whether or not they give rise to any tax risks.

By going through the three monthly Tax Risk Matrix update process you as business owner will also have additional insight into any emerging tax risks from the accounting treatment of income and expense items on your profit and loss monthly statement. If your business is starting to operate in other states beware of the extent of your physical presence in those other states as this may trigger sales tax and state tax commitments in those other states, as well as state tax issues.

Step required from you the business owner:

Have you questioned your accountant to make sure that you have considered all historical accounting problems that might cause tax risk yes/no

_____   _____

            Sign   Date

Have you questioned your accountant on any emerging tax risks from new income or expense entries on your profit and loss statement yes/no

_____   _____

            Sign   Date

TRM™ Step 7—Communication

Monthly communication will take place with your accountant to make sure that your Tax Risk Matrix is up to date. Stay connected to www. tax-Radar.com.

The moment that any contact is made with you by the IRS it is essential that through the tax-Radar™ program you immediately inform your accountant and tax-Radar™ representative, who will then put into action their methodology to represent you immediately.

Step required from you the business owner:

Will you ensure that if the IRS makes any contact with you, that you will immediately contact you accountant and tax-Radar™ representative yes/no

_____   _____
            Sign   Date

About the Author

Daniel N. Erasmus is an adjunct Professor of Law at Thomas Jefferson School of Law, San Diego, California. He was born on November 6, 1962, in what was then Rhodesia, now Zimbabwe. He qualified as an attorney and was admitted to practice as an attorney of the high court of South Africa in 1987. From then on he specialized in tax, dealing with multinational corporations in their planning, and then adversarial relationships with various tax authorities. He commenced practicing for his own account in 1993 and founded the successful www.taxriskmanagement.com and www.tax-Radar.com, today a multidisciplinary consulting firm, which assists its extensive client base, worldwide, in staying within the borders of the various complex tax laws but at the same time ensuring their exposure to tax is legitimately set to what the law prescribes as the minimum.

It was through his acting for multinationals in tax disputes that he developed a nose for the effect a constitution has on a country's tax laws. This knowledge he quickly developed into a formidable defense to any aggressive tax authority official seeking to bully his way to a quick revised assessment without making the effort to follow a very complex series of legal procedures, governed by the constitution, in doing so. The results for the taxpayers were remarkable. For the tax authorities, it was sometimes devastating, especially when their publicly announced goals were scarcely met in some cases. However, it became apparent to him that a higher road needed to be sought to address the constant waxing and waning of interaction between taxpayers and the tax authorities, especially as some of them were major tax contributors. And so a series of lectures was started some years ago on tax risk management TRM™ to teach taxpayers how to go about the process of a proactive TRM™ process, so as to avoid the painful process of being in a dispute with tax authorities. Yet with the same remarkable results previously achieved, this special report is the ultimate result.

This is the seventh special report or book the author has published. The first one was on VAT, the second special report was on CGT, the third special report, was on the Exchange Control and Tax Amnesty in South Africa, the fourth was the first edition of this book in South Africa, the fifth a children's story book, and the sixth, he co-authored the IBFD Tax Risk Management: From Risk to Opportunity.

He is registered to practice as an attorney in South Africa and practices in the USA as a foreign and international attorney. He is also near the completion of his PhD on constitutional law and tax, a project that has taken some eight years' research. As adjunct Professor of Law at the Thomas Jefferson School of Law he teaches International Tax Planning, Tax Risk Management, Tax Controversy and International Law aspects of Taxation. He is the founding editor of the magazine *TAXtalk*, hosted a weekly TV show called *Tax Issues* on a business satellite channel in Africa, and lectures extensively on tax risk management TRM™, structured finance, tax practice, transfer pricing, tax controversy, and other related topics, internationally.

The author resides between Atlanta, South Africa, and Florida, USA. He is an avid cyclist, amateur artist, photographer, and permanent student of tax and its side avenues.

Index

Made in the USA
Lexington, KY
16 May 2011